FROM PRISON TO REDEMPTION

Thomas L. Morrison, III

Kingdom Builders Publications LLC

Romans 8:28
And we know that all things work together for good for those who are called according to His purpose.

Joshua 1:9
Have not I commanded thee? Be strong and of a good courage; be not afraid neither be dismayed: for the Lord thy God is with thee whithersoever thou goest.

Romans 12:1
I beseech you, therefore, brethren, by the mercies of God,
That ye present your bodies a living sacrifice, holy, acceptable
Unto God, which, is your reasonable service.

Thomas L. Morrison, III

© 2019 Thomas L. Morrison, III
From Prison to Redemption
Kingdom Builders Publications, LLC

All rights reserved. No part of this book may be reproduced or transmitted in any form or by any means without written permission from the author.

Printed in the USA

ISBN
978-0-578-52816-8

Authored by
Thomas L. Morrison, III

Editor
Kingdom Builders Publications
Wanda Brown

Cover Design
LoMar Designs
ID 23214877 © Philcold | Dreamstime.com

Scripture use permitted
King James Version
New International Version
Amplified Version

This Book Belongs to

Thomas L. Morrison, III

DEDICATION

I dedicate this book to my wife. Tonya, I am thankful for you. A famous Proverbs quote, *"He who finds a wife finds a good thing, and obtains favor from the Lord."* You, Tonya, are bone of my bone and flesh of my flesh. I so love you babe. We've had our ups and downs but I thank the Lord that you stuck by me. You *are* my good thing. We were made for each other and I bless the Lord for you.

I give thanks for all of my children, both natural and by choice, this includes my stepchildren. To my natural children, Taryn, Taetiana, Alyssa, and Dashawn, I love all of you. I may not have gotten it right with your moms', but that doesn't stop me from getting it right with you. I also dedicate this book to the memory of my mother, Mrs. C. Jackson. I will forever love you; I miss you dearly. I wish you were here.

Thank you Eveta for your inspiration and the skill used to pen my story. I am grateful.

I dedicate this book to those who are in bondage mentally, generationally, spiritually and physically. It took deliverance for me to see that the unseen bondages were the root of all my problems. I pray that my book provides some guidance for you to see your way clearly.

I dedicate this book to the fivefold ministry (apostles, prophets, evangelists, pastors, and teachers), as well as deacons and other lay ministry leaders. While reading this book, I pray all will read with an ear to hear what the Lord is saying in these days.

I also dedicate this book to those who are still in the struggle. Those people who are in the streets (the prostitutes, the pimps, the drug addicts and drug dealers) can be some of the most faithful and most evangelistic members you can ever have in your church. These people personally know what the people are going through in the streets. Please know Jesus was attracted to the outcasts of society.

From Prison to Redemption

Thomas L. Morrison, III

TABLE OF CONTENTS

DEDICATION	IV
THE CHOSEN ONE	8
AN UNCONVENTIONAL CHILDHOOD	20
THE FEDS, MY MOM, AND ME	38
MY TEENAGE YEARS:	41
THE BEGINNING OF MY ADDICTIONS	41
THE EVERYDAY HUSTLE	52
COPING IN THE DOPE GAME	59
RUNNING FROM THE GAME	67
THE RAP GAME	70
THE CROSSROADS:	74
THE DAY EVERYTHING CHANGED	74
I FOUND MY BLOOD BROTHERS	80
THE RELATIONSHIP FROM HELL	84
MY OTHER MISTAKES	89
ADDICTIONS	94
RELAPSE	99
EPILOGUE	104
MORE ABOUT THE AUTHOR	106

THE CHOSEN ONE
Chapter One

While I was alone at home on a particular day, I decided to take a stroll in my neighborhood. The weather was mild with a slight wind. On this particular day, I was wearing short-sleeved shirt and slacks. The sky was blue, the birds were chirping, and the wind was blowing. Everything seemed to be right in my world. As I walked around my estate, and took everything in, I had to thank my Lord and Savior Jesus Christ. It was only the Lord who got me to this place in my life. This is my place of rest. *"Let us labour therefore to enter into that rest, lest any man fall after the same example of unbelief." - **(Hebrews 4:11)*** It takes faith and endurance to enter God's rest. Rest happens when you are acting in faith, depending on the will of the Lord and not yourself. Rest happens when you trust in the will of God for your life. Rest happens when you are honest with yourself, when you are able to confess your sins, both hidden and aware.

When I look in the mirror, I can barely recognize the man staring right back at me. I've wondered why I was chosen to do this work. I ask, *"Why me Lord?"* Why did God want me to be so transparent about my past and tell people about my life and what I went through? Who am I that you would be so mindful of me (*see Psalm 8:4*)?

Presently, I am a minister of the gospel of Jesus Christ. I

love ministering through gospel rap music. However, if people were to look at my past for reference, they'd most likely disqualify me as a minister. I am also a husband, father, grandfather and businessman. My heart is for the people on the streets because I know what they are going through. I am not the person I used to be. I actually know what it feels like to be homeless and on the streets. I am an ex-felon who was in and out of prison for 16 years. I am an ex-gangbanger who was often looking for my next hustle, my next score or an enemy to get even with. I put strongholds on entire neighborhoods. I was feared. I got people to do what I wanted them to do by any means necessary.

I am a recovering alcoholic and drug addict who went on binges for days at a time. As an ex-felon, I was so used to breaking laws and getting away with it until things caught up with me. As an ex-gangbanger and recovering drug addict, I discovered that a lot of people are judgmental toward people on the streets. I will tell you that unless you have walked in their shoes, you have no idea what they are going through or what got them there in the first place. I freely admit that I am not perfect, no one is. I admit that I have sinned and fallen short of the glory of God *(**Romans 3:23**)*. In order for true deliverance to take place, we must admit our sins and shortcomings. *If we say we have no sin, we deceive ourselves and the truth is not in us. If we confess our sins, God is faithful to forgive our sins and cleanse us from all unrighteousness.* – **1st John 1:8**

I chose to come forward to tell my story because there are people who do not know the lifestyle I led. They see a minister of the Gospel who likes to go to the streets with the Word of God. I am proof of God's grace, mercy and forgiveness. You could say I had a Damascus Road experience *(**See Acts 3:9**)*. When you read about Paul in the Bible, Paul persecuted the Christians because he thought his way was right and the Christians were wrong. Like

Paul, I thought my way of life was the right way. God was not pleased with the way I was living. Changes had to take place so I could move forward. Back in the day, my life was so much different from what it is now. My former life was nowhere near this peaceful or normal. It was filled with constant trouble and uncertainty. I lived the thug lifestyle. The street thug has a relentless spirit. There is no rest for the street thug. It was as if I was in a constant state of searching. Life was a constant struggle.

I was engaged in a tug of war. A part of me hungered and thirsted for the wrong things. However, the other part of me knew there was more to life than using drugs, gangbanging, and switching up women every chance I got. I searched for that something to make me feel good. Money, drugs and women oftentimes did the trick, but its thrills were temporary and lasted shorter than a N.Y. moment.

Back in my younger days, I was a risk taker and a force to be reckoned with. With emotional issues, anger sat at the root of my troubling state. Oftentimes, I took my anger out on lots of people. I used to act out of my emotions. *"Do not be quickly provoked in your spirit, for anger resides in the lap of fools."* **Ecclesiastes 7:9**

I had some ferocious and violent tendencies. I'd jack up anyone who I thought was trying to play me. I didn't hesitate to take my anger out on strangers and my many significant others. I shook many lives because of my anger. I have survived shoot outs and other hidden dangers. I wanted to hold on to the tangible, and money was my primary god back then. It was the thing I cared about most. Needless to say, I did not play when it came to my money, and because I often acted out of anger, I had to be on my guard. I carried a gun in my waist band. I constantly watched out for any revengers coming to get restitution on the ugliness of my past. I used to beat people up in the streets. I wasn't above pistol whipping a man just for kicks. It was all in my attitude.

My attitude had to change in order for my mind to be renewed. *"And be renewed in the spirit of your mind; and that ye put on the new man, which after God is created in righteousness and true holiness. Wherefore putting away lying, speak every man truth with his neighbor: for we are members one of another. Be ye angry, and sin not: let not the sun go down upon your wrath: Neither give place to the devil."* – **Ephesians 4: 23-26**

When you attempt to change your life, the devil will fight you every step of the way. It is not a physical fight; it is a spiritual fight. However, with prayer (constant relationship with God), fasting (bringing the flesh under subjection for a period from food, those old ways and thinking) and being in the Word, you can fight those old ways and go forth into those things the Lord has for you.

In order to genuinely change your attitude, you must change your mind and the way you go about doing things, you have to first be honest with yourself and those around you. It took a while for me to be honest with myself. I needed the Lord, Jesus in my life. *"If you confess with your mouth the Lord Jesus, and believe in your heart that God has raised him from the dead you will be saved."* – **Romans 10:9** I believe Jesus laid down His life for me. If it had not been for the Lord who was on my side, I shudder to think where I could be at this moment; I may have been deep in a forgotten grave.

Back in the day, I did so much dirt and caused so much hurt. Some days, I lived life as a father who was just trying to make ends meet for my small family. Other days, I took to the streets as a drug addict, looking for my next high. I roamed the streets for days searching for the best high I could find. Often times I did whatever was necessary to pay for the drugs that fueled my addictions. I lied, cheated, and stole to get drugs.

I've experienced some very low moments. At one of the lowest points of my life, I was homeless and hungry. I slept on a cardboard box underneath an interstate overpass and those nights were very cold.

Ironically, I was in prison, when I realized I'd had enough of living a life of instability and uncertainty. I turned to God in Prison. *"In all thy ways acknowledge Him and He will guide your hearts."* – **Proverbs 3:6** I had a change of heart while in bondage. Once those chains were broken, I never turned back. Although I still had struggles, I was determined not to turn back. I didn't always get it right but I'm in it to win it! I've made countless mistakes along the way, but I still look forward and embrace the blessings and assignments God has for my life.

It was God, His grace and His mercy that completely turned my life around for His purpose and glory. I found God (or rather, God found me) while I was in a six by eight feet prison cell. When He found me, I was at the end of my rope. I was at a crossroads in my life. I didn't know whether to go forward or turn and go backwards.

Those of you who have been in and out of the prison system know exactly what I am talking about. It is that point where going back to those old ways could mean death (mentally, spiritually and physically). A mental and spiritual death is worse than a physical death. When you are at a crossroad, you have a decision to make. Will you go forward into a new life? Will you stay in your comfort zone or will you go back to your old life? I had to make that decision and make it fast. There comes a point where you get tired of the old life. I will not lie to you, it was a struggle to stay on the straight and narrow, but I had to keep looking forward. *"Let your eyes look straight ahead; fix your gaze directly before you. Give careful though to the paths for your feet and be steadfast in all your ways. Do not turn to the right or the left, keep your foot from evil." –* **Proverbs 4:25-27 (NIV)** When you are trying to do right, you have to focus so that you can stay on the straight and narrow. *"Enter through the narrow gate and broad is the road that leads to destruction and many enter through it." –* **Matthew 7:13 (NIV)**

You cannot look to the right or look to the left. Even now, I have to constantly fight off those old thuggish ways (and staying away from those people who don't want to live right). That old thug often wants to come back and wreak havoc on my life. I am not perfect. To this day, I am still mending fences that were erected by my loved ones, my babies' mommas and others I've hurt. Oftentimes, I have to find myself in an Alcoholics Anonymous or a Narcotics Anonymous meeting just to stay clean. After the Lord came into my life, there were times when I relapsed back into heavy drug use, drinking and stinking ways of thinking. Yes, you can relapse mentally and it is just as bad as a physical relapse into drug use. However, with the help of the Lord and some of the ministers who have helped me, I have moved forward. Now, I am living my dream life.

If you had told me back then when I was in that prison cell I would become a successful gospel hip hop artist, who has toured the world, a minister of the gospel, a praise and worship leader, an advocate for the prevention of domestic violence, a productive member of society who meets with the mayor of his city for lunch, a mentor to troubled teens and children and a homeowner in a loving marriage to a supportive wife, I might have laughed at you and told you, you are completely out of your mind (after I called you everything but a child of God). These roles are a far cry from my former life. In order to move forward, the biggest change had to start in my mind. Sometimes, when you cannot see what is possible, the Lord will often use vessels that will help shine a light on things you cannot see.

When I was younger, anger, hatred, instability, drug addiction, failure and sinfulness were my reality. However, because of Jesus, a transformation has taken place in my life. Now joy, love, stability, sobriety, success and holiness are my reality. I have been clothed with the garment of praise (*see Isaiah 61:3*). It is so amazing how when you fully commit your life to the Lord and His word, He can totally transform you and your circumstances. When the Lord came into my life, He literally turned it around. Life as I knew it started to change and I could not understand it at first. When you are so used to doing wrong, right often looks and feels weird. Every area of my life was impacted by the love I experienced from God's people.

The jail term: *three hots and a cot* were no longer sufficient. What I used to get away with, didn't work anymore. My gang banging didn't bring me any joy anymore. Pimping did not gratify me nor did my reoccurring drug habit sustain me. Even the women could not satisfy me. They could not compare or come close to the love I was getting from Jesus.

When you invite the Lord into your life, you begin to realize many new things. I had to sit down and examine my life. I had to get God's Word into my spirit. I had to become a doer of the Word. As I begin to read and study the Word of God, I tried putting Him first in my life. I learned these points: 1. I wasn't perfect, 2. Problems and curses were all connected to sin, 3. There were promises from God for His people. I was still getting use to this newness, so I'd still slip back in disobedience. There were numerous situations and generational curses plaguing my life and it kept my family and me at odds and in constant turmoil.

I aspired to be one of the greatest rap artists of all times. As a matter of fact, I almost had a record deal on a major rap label. I ended up messing that up and losing that deal because I was still stuck in the past. Losing that deal ended up being a good thing for me. Later I found out that deal could have sent me to a point of no return; literally selling my soul to the devil just to sustain its evils.

I was addicted to cocaine, crack and weed. I kept going in and out of prison, sometimes on purpose, just to survive. I was a very violent man. I was quick to react and I asked questions in the wake of the aftermath. *"My dear brothers and sisters take note of this everyone should be quick to listen, slow to speak, and slow to become angry,"* — ***James 1:19***

When I was on the streets, I definitely got angry very quickly. I was feared. I was a lost soul, but when I started calling on the Lord, seeking Him through prayer and reading His Word, He gave me multiple chances to get it right. He changed my rap game. I went from singing about the everyday street hustle, prison, sex, women, money, and drugs to singing about salvation and the cleansing power of the blood of Jesus. The transformation was not because of anything I did. It was God's sovereign grace and mercy that saved me and set me free. My mindset started to transform. I went from eternal death to everlasting life. I went from Prison to Redemption. I am not a perfect man, but the Love of Jesus makes me a forgiven man.

I am coming forward to share my testimony as a cautionary

tale. I want others to be saved before it is too late. In order to help people become saved and delivered, I had to come forth and testify about the goodness and mercy of Jesus Christ. To those men and women who are still living in sin on the streets, I will simply tell you time is running out. You cannot continue to live just any way you want. The Word of God says the wages of sin is death (*see Romans 6:23*). Hell is a real place. Some of you think you know the place well already, but you actually don't. I am warning you so I can save you from the pain of paying for your sins while you have the time to repent. Warning comes before destruction. If you are still out there manipulating, killing, stealing, and cheating, then you are on the road to self-destruction. This story serves as your warning to get it right. Let this story serve as your final wakeup call. Let this book help you. This is your chance to allow God to help you get a new life. If you heed to the message in this book, you can change the trajectory of your destiny and your family's.

    Many of you are as I was; a slave to the streets. You are mothers and fathers, some with young children and some with adult children. God blessed you and made you fruitful despite it all. Truth be told, many of us were blest with children out of some of the craziest situations. I know I was blessed and I love every one of my children. I will share many of those crazy situations in this book. You can use this book as a guide to seek the opportunities to live your best life right and break the generational strongholds that are keeping your family in constant crisis. Struggles with lust, anger and rejection were at the root of many generational curses that plagued my mom, my sisters and me. I am a living witness that prayer and supplication changes things. If your children are adults, you could be a grandparent, so it's time for you to surrender, get into your prayer closet (your secret place), pray to the Most-High God and ask Him to change things for your future generation.

Prayer provides you a secret place to abide in. *"He that dwelleth in the secret place of the Most-High shall abide under the shadow of the Almighty. I will say of the Lord, He is my refuge and my fortress: my God; in him will I trust." – **Psalms 91:1-2***

The Lord is my strength. I am nothing without Him. He gives me direction, but I have to pray and read the Word of God daily for the fight ahead. I know while you're reading my book you may be wondering what to do next in a seemingly hopeless situation. I sat where you are sitting. There's no getting away from God. I wouldn't want to get away from Him. *"If I ascend up into heaven: if I make my bed in hell, behold, thou art there." – **Psalm 139:8 (KJV)*** Always remember God is for you.

When living the street life, you make friends and you make enemies, but you have to be careful. You have to watch your back for enemies; which for the most part, are the cops. Living like that is not a good life, it's like prison. There are millions of men and women out there hustling in the street game because they feel as though they have no choice. Look I get it - people don't know what it is like to need food or diapers for your baby, or quick money because you need your rent paid, immediately. Some people don't know what it's like to make things happen. When I was living that street life there was constantly a sense of urgency. Those food stamps and Section 8 don't seem to cut it at times. You say to yourself, "I'm supposed to be a man. I'm supposed to be the provider. I have to make it happen." I was faithful about making those *Benjamins*, but at what cost? A lot of times I risked my life for the hustle and instead of a thanks, I got the cold shoulder from my girl.

If you have this book in your hands, then it is not too late to change your ways and come to Christ. *"And they overcame him by the blood of the Lamb, and by the word of their testimony; and they loved not their lives unto the death." – **Revelation 12:11*** I had to give up my life so I would gain it back (***Matthew 16:25***). I am a living testimony of the goodness and mercy of Jesus Christ. There are various men and women who are walking the streets, sitting in prison cells, hospital wards, crack houses, and whore houses that are in a dismal fog; the way I used to be. They constantly find themselves thirsting for things that do not give them long term satisfaction. Many have given up on life, but I say hold on, it's not too late to get it right.

Society said that the odds were stacked against me. I grew up not knowing who my real father was. The man I thought was my father was a womanizer and adulterer. When I met my real father, it frankly was by coincidence.

My mother served as a drug mule (carrier) for several gangs. One of my sisters was a drug addict and prostitute, and she ended up losing her life because of it. These were the role models I had. They showed me the wrong way to live. It wasn't until the Lord Jesus came into my life that I gained a better role model and discovered my life had a greater purpose. As a father, I strive daily to be a better role model to my children and the kids I mentor in the community.

I have a relationship with all of my children and plan to keep it that way until I go to my heavenly home. *"What is impossible with men is not impossible with God, because with God all things are possible" – (**Matthew 19:26 NIV**)*. The old man within me had to die so that my new man could be born and my new life could begin. *"Do not be conformed to the pattern of this world but be ye transformed by the renewing of your mind that ye may prove what is that good and acceptable and perfect will of God." – **Romans 12:2*** I had to submit to God so His work could begin. It is not over by a long shot. Transformation takes consistent work. I had to renew my mind in Christ Jesus in order to become the ***Sanktified Soulja*** whom God has called me to be. It was a process to renew my mind and spirit. *"Commit thy Works unto the Lord and your thoughts will be established." –* **Proverbs 16:3** Change takes commitment. I have to go through the process each and every day. You must be determined for the commitment! I had to in order to get to where I am.

Here is your official alarm clock! I want the story of my former life to serve as a wakeup call for someone who is going down the same path of life I was on. People who have lived through similar situation as I did, but some never lived to tell the story. Yet, Jesus gave me mercy. He truly redeemed a wretch like me. He sent some people into my life who saw potential in me. These people encouraged me and cheered me on. They encouraged me to keep the faith and pursue my dreams. He sent me ministers, pastors, prophets, managers and marketing agents who believed in my unique ministry.

These people helped me to bring the message of the gospel to a new audience around the world. Jesus also allowed me to find a strong, extraordinary, and beautiful woman, who I now call my wife. She is a true helpmate in every regard. She fell in love with the Christ within me.

FOCUS SCRIPTURE

Jeremiah 29:11- I know the thoughts that I think towards you says The Lord; thoughts of peace and not of evil to Give you a future and a hope.
1 Samuel 12:16 - Now then stand still and see this great thing the Lord is about to do before your eyes.

AN UNCONVENTIONAL CHILDHOOD
Chapter Two

I was born in a big city. Although I currently live in a small rural area, I am a city boy at heart. At first, my childhood was typical of many children in the urban cities. I was born into a single parent household. My mother had five children (four girls and one boy). All five of us had different fathers, many of which were absent from our lives. This fact, in itself, was the main source of problems and stress for my mother. She had a lot of financial pressures on her. She had to pay the lights, water and mortgage by herself. Sometimes a few of the dads wanted to be fathers and slide Momma a couple of bucks here and there, but it was never enough.

I didn't care for Thomas Morrison, Sr., the man that my family told me was my father. I know that's not a real *Christian* thing to say, but I have to be real with what I was feeling at the time. I was told by family members that Thomas Morrison, Sr., was repeatedly angry and he recurrently overreacted. He got into lots of fights with Momma and that's why he and Momma could not stay together. The one time I remember seeing him did not go well. He came to see me and Momma at the house. I was outside, in front of the house, playing with my friends. I was having fun. For some unknown reason, he walked up to me and slapped me down in the street in front of everybody. I guess he thought that I disrespected him in some way. He wanted to assert his parental authority over me. He told me when I saw him, I was to drop everything and go to him immediately.

"You will respect me," He said.

I looked at him like he was crazy. He wasn't around enough for me to actually show respect. From that point forward, I sincerely didn't care if he came to see me or not. I honestly didn't want to see him. I didn't bother to pursue a relationship with him once I got into my teenage years.

You have to be a strong woman to raise five children on your own. Even though she was a single mother, she provided for us and did her best to make sure we had clean clothes to wear, a nice house to stay in and food to eat. If you didn't do what Momma asked you to do the first time, you'd be disciplined. She used belts, shoes, brooms, or extension cords; it did not matter. If you made her mad by not doing what she told you to do the second time, you'd surely be punished.

In the beginning, Momma was especially hard on my older sisters. She was very stern with them. They had to have good grades in school. She didn't let them experience a lot of things that girls their age in urban areas experienced. For my sisters, dating was out of the question for a long time. If they went to the store, they had to get back quickly or she went looking for them. Nevertheless, my sisters managed to find ways to rebel against my mom. They often snuck into the garage and smoke cigarettes when Mom wasn't home.

For the first eight years of my life, I don't know how we made it. All I know is that my mom was a hustler. She did what it took to make money. Momma held down some very good jobs at first. She once worked as a secretary for the mayor and then for the police department for a short time. One of my sisters said

Momma went to the police academy for a few years (that's probably why the cops gave her a hard time later on). Momma drove the metro city bus for a while. I remember riding the bus as she drove.

My sisters liked doing girlie things. When they weren't keeping the house clean or doing other chores, they enjoyed playing with dolls and played dress up. Momma forbade playing with makeup. It was out of the question. As a boy, growing up with all girls wasn't much fun. Fortunately, I had boys around my neighborhood to play with. A couple of them grew up in the houses around mine. We played a lot in the streets in front of my house. There were many days we played baseball, football and basketball. We played with our toy soldiers and ran around a lot. We rode our bikes and met up at different spots. I especially loved playing with the boys that lived right across from my Grandmother Morrison's house. There were two brothers who lived there and their father was best friends with my father. We did some crazy things at times. One day, on a dare, I laid in the middle of the street in the dark. Cars just drove over me but didn't touch or hit me. The cars didn't even scrape me. The boys and I tripped out because that was a stupid thing to do. I know now God, in his sovereign grace, protected me at times when I didn't make wise decisions.

Although I had fun as a child, I remember some embarrassing moments growing up. I remember playing little league football and Momma brought me a banana bike so I could go back and forth to practice. One day, before going to little league practice, I got so hungry and wanted a snack. So, before practice, I went to the corner store on my banana bike. I brought this oversized long pepperoni stick; it was two feet long and it was so delicious. I finished the entire stick and it actually made me full.

After I finished the pepperoni stick, I went to football practice. Practice went fine but unfortunately; nature took its course while I was running around and playing on the field with the other boys. I had to go to the bathroom so bad, I could barely hold it. Then, a bunch of boys fell on me and it happened. I boo booed on myself. Then one of the little boys said, "Ewww, someone fell in boo boo." Everybody got up." As all of them got up off me, I walked away. They pointed at me and said, "Ewww, You got boo boo all over your pants. Ewww!" I started crying because I was so embarrassed. I called my mom and she came and got me and took me home. After I got home, I took a bath and changed my clothes. She could tell I was still embarrassed by what occurred. I heard Momma say, "Don't worry about it. They can laugh at you if they want to. It could happen to them. It could happen to anybody. You are still a big boy". Moments like this actually made me realize how much I loved my momma. She comforted me so much in my life. She was a good mom, and although she wasn't perfect, she gave her children assurance, even in times of trouble. She often made me feel at ease. She had countless problems, but regardless of all the problems she had, one thing was commonly prevalent; she loved and cared for all of her children.

    Everything started out normal, at first. Momma's true problems weren't exposed. She hid her problems from us for a while. For instance, her drug use wasn't a problem at first. All she did was smoke a little weed from time to time. She was able to hold a job and maintain a household full of children. However, her personal circumstances got worse. As her drug abuse worsened, it affected everything and everyone around her. The first sign things were going downhill was when Momma lost her job with the City Metro. Then, she started staying out to all times of night. She came home rambling her words. The men she associated with were not exactly upright citizens. Then, the household suffered. As the money diminished, food became scarce, cut-off notices were on the door from the power company.

To make money, she started running an after-hours night club in our house. Around 10 pm every night, when all of the other bars and clubs closed, Momma opened up our house to people who wanted to hang out late at night. As children, we had to go to bed once the people started coming over. The afterhours club often brought some very shifty people into our house. There was gambling, music, dancing, and drinking. The smell of weed was in our bedrooms. We heard all sorts of things going on in the front like car doors slamming as people came and went. Momma didn't close down until the sun was coming up. After everyone left, Momma slept for several hours. The money was good, for a time, but it wasn't meant to last.

Things started to get rough at the afterhours club. People got into arguments and fights. Drunks urinated in the front yard. It got to the point where Mom couldn't control her guests. After the neighbors complained about the noise and threatened to call the cops, Momma had to shut the club down for good. With five children to house, clothe, feed and care for, Momma had no choice but to go on welfare. The state took great care of us. We had a lot of food in the refrigerator. We had all the things we needed.

After a while, food became scarce again and the cut-off notices were back on the door. Eviction notices were on the door when we got home from school. We saw our Momma sleep at odd times of the day and out in the streets all times of night. Soon, we started finding the needles, the drugs and the dope in her purse. Now we knew for sure Momma had become a drug addict. Her drug abuse went from bad to worse.

Things at our house changed drastically. My sisters, fed up with my momma's rules, completely broke out of the house. They stayed out to all times of night and often stayed out for days at a time. One sister became a prostitute at the age of 12 to support herself and another starting hustling (selling cocaine). Even with them doing things for money, it wasn't enough. There were times when we found ourselves poor, homeless and on the streets. Momma often mismanaged the welfare money by using the rent money, food stamps or any other funds she received to buy drugs and dope. We went through eviction after eviction from our homes. We often stayed in shelters for warmth and comfort, but we had to change shelters frequently. First, we got comfortable at the one in midtown, then, a couple of days later we had to move and go downtown or the next city over. There were times my sisters and I went to sleep in fear.

I grew up with no father figure to guide me. Thomas Morrison, Sr., the man who I thought was my father, was never there for me. He rejected me as his son (I did not find out why until I was a grown man). Therefore, I had no fatherly protection. Truth be told, at this point in my life, I barely had motherly protection (although, she did the best she could under the circumstances). Things slowly went further downhill as Momma became more unstable. My mother became a very troubled woman. She turned to drugs, dope and pills to ease the anxiety caused by her choice of men and her decisions in life. She served as a drug mule. Many of the drug dealers paid Momma with drugs. She took a lot of risks carrying those drugs.

The 70's and 80's were a different time. The people we knew back then, dealt with turmoil and problems differently. Instead of talking things out or kneeling to pray about their issues, people lit up a joint, took a drink, snorted a line of cocaine, smoked a lot of crack, and anything else to ease the pain. My momma's drug addiction did not start overnight. It started over a number of years, stemming from all of the problems she faced.

As Momma's problems got bad, her children's situations got worse. I managed to get myself into a lot of trouble. I became a very curious kid. I developed a fetish for looking up the dresses and skirts of little girls and women. I often acted inappropriately towards females. This behavior stayed with me for a very long time. I had to be delivered from my perverted behavior long after I was a grown man. For quite some time, self-control was an issue for me.

When children often try to do whatever they want to do and not listen, adults often use fear as an effective tool to deter children from doing crazy things. Fear was often used to keep us kids from getting into trouble. My Auntie Ellen had a house overlooking this big field. I remember her house fondly. Her house was often one of the safe places my sisters and I had as kids. Aunt Ellen's house was full of the peace and normalcy we as children, barely knew. Our aunts and uncle's houses were nothing like our home. They had lights, running water, food and stability. Most of their homes were orderly, full of love and warmth. My aunts and uncles took pride in caring for their families. From what I could tell, the majority of them led happy and productive lives. They worked regular jobs and were in stable marriages. They cooked dinner and sat around the table to eat like normal people.

As children, my sisters and I often dealt with lights being turned off. We also had to deal with a lot of strange men coming in and out of our home. When we were evicted, we had to deal [with living homeless, in and out of shelters. We constantly changed schools and barely had time to make friends or learn. We had to deal with a lot of drug use by my mom and her companions, a lot of violence and outright dysfunction.

Our Auntie Ellen's house was a refuge for us. As children, the only downside of going to my Auntie Ellen's house was where we had to cross a field and walk close to Old Man Hanks house. Old Man Hanks was a scary looking ol' man. His hair and beard were white and he often looked disheveled. In reality, Old Man Hank was just a quiet, old man whom kept to himself. He wore this gangster style hat, which was laid to the side. He did not have any family or friends around. His house was a run-down shack at the edge of the large field which looked haunted and scary. Mulberry bushes were by his house. He stood on his leaning porch and just stared at the children. A lot of times, when children got too close to his house (to pick the mulberries), he came off the porch, walking with his cane, to close the gate and keep the children out. Many children tried to get mulberries from the bush near his house. When the children saw him, they quickly ran to the other side as fast as they could, screaming as they ran. We were scared to walk this field because of Old Man Hanks. There was an urban legend which said; if Old Man Hanks ever caught you in his yard, he kept you forever. Old Man Hanks' yard was right by the field. Sometimes children dared each other to run as close as they could to the *'man of the spooky legend's'* yard. Many children, who were thrill-seekers, ran around Old Man Hanks yard and ran back out without getting caught. The stories were just fables that people made up for entertainment sake. However, children, like me, took stories like that to heart.

The kids, I went to school with, didn't make life easy for me. They often teased me because they knew about a lot of the stuff Momma was doing in the streets. Momma boosted (stole) whatever she could in order to sell on the streets, and she boosted anything she could get her hands-on like clothes, food, and cigarettes.

Momma made a lot of money as a drug mule for many gangbangers, dealers, and anyone in between who wanted to use her to transport drugs for them. She started hanging out with these hardcore gangsters in the clubs. These hardcore gangsters were nothing to play with. The men my mom had relationships with were very abusive and had explosive tempers. One man in particular (we shall call him Psycho), was very violent and creepy. He was good at first, polite and gentle toward Momma. Then he got creepy. Psycho's sister warned Momma about him, but Momma didn't listen. She told Momma her brother nearly beat his previous girlfriend to death with an iron, while she was sleeping, and he wasn't charged. Why this guy wasn't in a jail cell for what he did shocked my sisters and me. Then, I realized, during that time period, men could get away with a lot of things (because later in my early adulthood, I did get away with a lot of my violence toward women. I am very sorry about that).

It wasn't long before he set his sights on Momma. He stalked her. She got an order of protection from the police, but it didn't stop Psycho from harassing her. He became very possessive and showed up uninvited to the house or at the club Momma frequented. At night, when he thought everyone was sleeping, he peeked into our windows to see if Momma was there. Many times, my sisters and I went to bed in fear, wondering what could happen to Momma while we were sleeping. There were times when Psycho caught up with her and fought her in the streets. Our Momma came home bruised from his physical attacks. She was so afraid of him. She had to watch her back whenever she went out. Finally, my sisters and I had had enough of this creep terrorizing our mother, so we took it upon ourselves to protect her. It was time Psycho learned a valuable lesson; nobody was going to mess with our momma and get away with it.

One day, he got really bold and had the nerve to break into our house. Momma wasn't home, she was at the club. That night, my sisters and I were ready for him. As he walked down the hall in the dark, we switched on the lights. We ambushed him and proceeded to take all of our frustrations out on him. We gave him a true beat down. We punched, stomped and berated him. We beat him up so bad, he ran out of the house and never came back. We all slept very well in the house after that. Psycho thought because there wasn't a grown man living in the house, he could do whatever he wanted and get away with it. We showed him! From that day on, our mom, nor we lived in fear. That boosted our confidence from that point on, and if any man put his hands on our Momma, we physically fought to defend her.

After the Psycho incident, the caliber of men Momma choose to deal with got worse. Many of these men introduced her to a lot more drugs. As a result, Momma came home very high. Oftentimes, these men were heartless and very violent. Some of these men had no value on human life. She lost many friends and associates because of all the violence and mayhem these men left in their wake.

One night, I heard Momma come in the front door. I was happy to see she got home safe. As I peeked around the corner, I saw Momma sitting on the couch. She had a look of shock on her face. Her appearance was disheveled. Her face and her eyes were beet red because she was crying. She was nervous and a bit shaky. She was chain smoking cigarettes back to back. As I approached her, I could see she was visibly shaken. I asked, "What happened

Momma, what's wrong?" She looked at me, shook her head, and took a long drag off of her cigarette. She told of her close friend Bill, who was shot and killed in the club that night. I was stunned. I asked, what happened? Momma said, "We were just sitting there in the club. The music was playing and everyone was doing their own thing, minding their own business, and having a good time. Bill and I were just chilling and drinking. Nobody was bothering anyone. This guy just walked up to Bill. He said, 'Hey Bill.' As Bill looked up, the guy just pulls his gun out and just blew Bill's head right off. And just like that, Bill was gone off this earth. I was right beside Bill when the guy just blows his head clean off. Bill is gone. Just like that. I saw Bill's spirit just leave his body. What was scary was the guy just walked off like nothing happened." She paused, "I don't know why he let me live. He just walked away. He didn't even glance at me."

When the cops came to the club, they questioned Momma extensively, but Momma said she didn't see anything because the club was real dark. I remembered feeling bad about Bill getting killed. Momma and Bill were pretty tight. Bill was a great guy, but like all of the men in my momma's life, he was unarguably messed up on drugs and alcohol.

She was real torn up about her friend losing his life like that. Momma cried for weeks and drank herself to sleep. The image of Bill's murder constantly played out before her eyes. It was years before she could move past it. I remember feeling so sorry for all she went through that night, but I felt so relieved the man who shot Bill did not kill my momma. With all of my momma's drug use, I loved her and I still needed her.

My mother used the dope, the pills, and the alcohol to cope and numb the pain of what she witnessed. When she was sober, she had many nightmares of Bill's untimely and unforgettable death. She woke up in the middle of the night screaming. It startled my sisters and me to the point where we could not go back to sleep. The tormenting dreams my mom had were also tormenting me. I worried about her. It just got to the point where the drugs became the lord of her life.

When you use drugs and alcohol, they draw you in. The flesh starts to crave the drugs and alcohol. Oftentimes, if the person is not strong enough, they are powerless to fight against it alone. When you are dealing with the flesh, the flesh wants to do whatever it wants to do. *"Be sober-minded; be watchful. Your adversary the devil prowls around like a roaring lion, seeking someone to devour." 1st* **Peter 5:8** Often times, in motion pictures, they want to glamorize drug use. I assure you, there is nothing glamorous about using drugs.

No matter what my mother did, I loved her, but often times, I was disrespectful towards her, and that's because I was very spoiled and wanted my way. Times in, and times out, I yelled at her hoping she would change, but having a mom who was a drug dealer was, I thought at the time pretty cool. She was somewhat of a heroine to me. Later in my teen and young adult years, I disrespected her to the point where I thought it was ok to smoke dope with her. No matter what I did or said, my mother was my biggest cheerleader. She believed in me regardless of the things we went through. She consistently encouraged me to do better. She encouraged me to continue to pursue my rap career. I wish I could take back all of the times I disrespected her. I wish she could come back.

Momma turned to a life of crime to fund her drug addiction, and because of her life of crime, my momma was constantly on the run from the cops. As a family, we were constantly on the run with her. While my sisters went to be with their fathers, I came home and had to immediately pack up what I could, to go on the run with Momma. I got used to traveling and hiding in different cities as a boy. We had to constantly be on our guard at all times. We had to be smart about doing a lot of things.

I became very street savvy because of the things I went through as a kid. I learned how to spot an undercover cop just by looking at him or her. I learned how to hustle on the streets as a young boy. I had to grow up fast. I had to be like that because I never knew when the cops came to get my mother and haul her away to jail.

No matter how much drugs Momma did, she was still concerned about her children. There was this one time my mom got me one of those leather bomber jackets for my birthday. It was genuine leather, soft and smooth to the touch. The jacket was *really nice*. It looked very expensive. I wore the jacket to school and a lot of people told me I looked good in the jacket, especially this girl I had a major crush on. She absolutely loved the jacket. One of the things we did as kids was switch clothes. She wore my jacket and I wore hers. Her jacket was slightly small on me, but that did not matter. It was just the feeling of wearing something that belonged to your crush. At the end of the school day, we hugged and kissed.

I made my way back to my apartment in the projects. When I got close to the apartment, there were a bunch of police cars in front of the building. I hated cops. Instinctively, I decided to take the back way to the apartment so I could avoid the cops in the front, just in case they decided to question me. The apartment pool was in the back of the building. I crossed by the pool cabana.

There were a bunch of bushes there by the pool. Then all of a sudden, I heard somebody say, "Tommy Boy." Only a couple of people called me that. One of them was this guy named Garry who was messing around with my mom at the time. Garry was a good guy but he was so messed up on crack and cocaine. He did a lot of stuff like boost and shop lift like my mother. Garry called me from the bushes. He said Tommy Boy three times. I kept looking around to see who was calling me.

Garry said, "Psst, over here in the bushes, it's me Garry." I was shocked and amazed he was in the bushes.

I said, "What are you doing in there?"

Garry said, "The cops are all over your apartment looking through all of your mom's stuff. Where's that jacket your mom got you for your birthday."

I said, "I don't have it right now. The girl I have a mad crush on switched jackets, but I can get it back tomorrow."

He said, "Boy, you just saved your mom's life. The cops are looking through the apartment trying to find that jacket. If they would have found it, they might have taken your mom to jail."

I asked, "Why didn't she just buy it?"

Garry said, "She didn't have the money. She loves you. She didn't want to let her baby boy down." I was frantic and relieved at the same time. I told Garry I was going up to the apartment.

As I made my way to the apartment, I was nervous. Cops were all over the place. I finally got to the apartment. As I went inside, the cops were surrounding Momma while she was sitting down on the couch. My sisters weren't home at the time. She looked up at me and then looked back down. As I went into the living room, I saw one of the police officers who recognized me. He stopped me and asked me where my other jacket was? I was wearing the white one I borrowed from the girl.

I said, "I don't have any other jacket."

He said, "That jacket is kind of small on you."

I abruptly told him, "This is the only jacket I have. We don't have a lot of money like that."

He looked as if he believed me. He said to the rest of the cops, "I think we are through here. Ok boys let's wrap it up and go." The cops seemed disappointed. They started getting their stuff together and leaving the apartment.

When the last cop left out and closed the door, my mother had this look of relief on her face. She reached out to me and hugged me undeniably tight. She said, "I love you so much. You actually saved me. You saved my life. If they had found that jacket, they might have taken me away for a long time." As she continued to hug me, Momma said, "now, go and get whatever you can fit into a bag. I have a warrant in another county. When they figure that out, they will come right back to get me." (This was when you had to look in each individual county system to check for warrants. Now, it is a central system).

We got all of our stuff together and hurried out of there and found our way to the car. Once Mom and I picked up what we could carry, she sent me to go get Garry. He picked up whatever he could carry in his hands. None of us had a suitcase. After we had what we needed, all of us hurried down the stairs.

Momma drove a 1979 Plymouth Fury back then. We all piled into the Fury. Momma wanted to speed in order to hurry up and get out of the apartment complex before the cops came back for her. There were a few speed bumps. She was going over the speed bumps doing 30 miles per hour. All of us were bouncing up in our seats. We finally got to the last stop sign. As we looked back, we saw the cops coming back to our building, five to six police cars deep. As we saw them going into the building, Momma looked in the rear-view mirror made a quick left turn at the stop sign. We hopped right on the interstate.

We drove for miles and miles. It was snowing hard that day but we didn't stop. We drove until we were few states over. We went to my Uncle Pap's house. We hid out with him and my cousins for a couple of months.

When we weren't on the run with her, she dropped us off to one of our aunts or uncles. Not seeing my momma was very hard. It was difficult not knowing where she was or if she was ok, but Mom was a natural hustler and knew what to do to survive. Oftentimes, when my mom dropped us off, it was a blessing. My aunts and uncles gave us refuge, away from all of the drug use, violence and police trouble my mom went through.

After a few months, Momma, Garry and I left Uncle Pap's house. We drove to another state where we stayed for a few months. One day, we all got hungry and went to the pizza place which was only a few feet from our house. We all sat down to eat. Momma's man, Garry was staying with us at the time. Garry taught me a lot about street hustling and street knowledge. He taught me how to sell dope and he showed me how to make chump change on the street. Chump change was about $200 to $300 in one day. He taught me how to do the three-cup game with the beans under the cups. He taught me a lot about con games and games of manipulation like the Three Card Molly. At his core, Garry was a good man and he taught me a lot of stuff. Learning a lot of these things helped me to survive during some rough times on the streets. While Garry was a good man, he was messed up pretty bad on cocaine. Everything valuable he had, went up his nose. He was so strung out; he could hardly hold down a job. He often hustled to survive and to buy his drugs.

As we were eating our pizza, I saw there was this white man in a long black trench coat. He had been standing on the other side of the parking lot for quite a while. The man kept looking at us as we sat inside the restaurant. As we were sitting and eating, I could not help but to keep looking at the man. I said, "Momma, that's the police." (as a little boy, I had a way of being able to tell if a person was a cop or not. I had to develop a nose for the police at an early age).

My momma said, "Boy, you don't know what you are talking about. That is not the police."

I snapped back, "Momma that is the police." Just then, another man came into the store. He said something to the store manager. He glanced over at us briefly and went back out the door.

About fifteen to twenty minutes later, the store manager came over to our table, and said, "Ma'am, the FBI is outside. They told me to tell you they are here to arrest you and you need to follow these directions. Number one, you need to send your son outside because they have a plane at the International Airport ready to fly him back to the city with an escort (already I wasn't feeling this because I had to get on the plane by myself). Number two, if you try to run, they will shoot you."

I looked at my mom and said "Momma, see I told you that was the police." I just started crying because I knew it was a wrap. I knew they were about to take my momma away to jail and I wouldn't be able to be with her for a while. I had to get on a plane and fly back to the city to my family.

I lost a lot of trust in my momma that day. I trusted her to protect me and to keep me safe and I trusted her to be there for me. Now, here I am in another state, far away from my other family, in the snow and the Feds are going to take me back to the city. They took my mom away I was crying a lot. It was one of the most terrifying times of my life. I was so afraid of never seeing my mother again. They had my Uncle Danny waiting at The City International Airport to pick me up.

FOCUS SCRIPTURE

Exodus 20:12 Honor thy father and thy mother: that thy days may be long upon the land which the Lord thy God giveth thee.

Proverbs 22:6 Train up a child in the way that he should go and when he is old, he will not depart from it

THE FEDS, MY MOM, AND ME
Chapter Three

Staying with my Uncle Danny was a bad experience for me. It started off bad because when I got on the plane, the FEDS did not give me a chance to pack any clothes. I only had the clothes on my back. In order to have clean clothes, I had to wear my little cousin's clothes. They were a little younger than me so I naturally couldn't fit their clothes. They had me getting clothes at the Salvation Army.

As small children, we loved Uncle Danny and he loved us. He provided for us. He made sure we had food to eat. He and his wife made sure we had a home to go to. He was our little league football coach. I had a lot of fun playing little league football. However, as an older child, living with him was like being in prison. He gave me my first taste of what it was like to be in the state pen. Uncle Danny was very stern and strict. He disciplined us for the slightest infraction. He raised us and his own children in a very militant environment; early to bed, early to rise. Uncle Danny's house felt more like a county lock up than a home. I hated being there. Mentally and physically, staying at Uncle Danny's became daunting.

We all stayed in the same room, boys and girls. I was hungry at Uncle Danny's. It seemed like I could never get enough food to eat. He fed us to only three very small meals a day. We could not get any more food, even if we asked.

While I stayed with Uncle Danny, I was often treated like an outsider. All of the other kids used to talk bad about my mom, because of what they heard the adults saying. Unfortunately, the things they were saying were true.

A few months after I got to Uncle Danny's house, I turned 11 years old. A couple of weeks later, my momma came to get me. Momma served six months in jail. They didn't keep her long. I was so happy to be getting out of Uncle Danny's house. I was so happy to see my momma and go back to the city. When we got back, Momma didn't have any money or a place to stay. The apartment complex had evicted her several months back, so, because of the lack of money, our family ended up in a city shelter.

As a boy, I was scared to be in the shelter, but the Lord was with us. Momma's family shunned her and barely gave her any financial help. The good thing was while she was in prison, she had time to dry out from all of the drugs and alcohol. I had my momma back for a while. She even worked for a time, but her sobriety was short lived.

Momma never had a problem getting a man, but she habitually had problems keeping a good man. The ones which were bad stayed for a while. When we were living in the shelter, Momma met a man named Bob. He was a bum who was living on the streets. Bob was struggling with an illness and for some reason Momma took a lot of pity on him and became very attracted to him. We were living in temporary housing and she took Bob in, cleaned him up and got him healthy again. Bob was grateful. In the midst of it all, they fell in love with each other. Momma and Bob got married down at the city hall several months after meeting each other.

Bob was a good man in many ways. He provided a tad bit of normalcy and stability for Momma. Together, they were able to get a place and get on their feet. Their normal life was short lived as Bob turned out to be a very bad influence for her. When he was around, Momma became high by doing a lot of cocaine, and drinking a lot of alcohol.

MY TEENAGE YEARS: THE BEGINNING OF MY ADDICTIONS
Chapter Four

My teenage years were just as messed up (if not much more) as my early childhood. My sisters and I became heavily involved with drugs and alcohol. Even now though I am clean and sober, I still have to acknowledge that I am a recovering alcoholic and drug addict. I say *recovering* because it is a daily commitment, I have to have so I won't relapse.

Many of my addictions started because of constant rejection. My sisters and I followed in my mother's alcoholic, sex and drug addicted footsteps. One of my sisters walked the whore stroll (prostitution) to feed herself and her addictions.

Many of my family members and closest friends were known gang members. I hung out with a lot of gang members before I actually became one of them. For gang members, submission is a tough thing to do. Most of the people I knew back in the day joined a gang to be a part of a family. It is sad, but of a true reality, this still goes on today. I was one of the young men who was lost. Joining a gang back then was not like it is now. Today, most times, gangs beat their members in. Some gangs make potential members go and commit a felony. The gang I became a part of watched me from afar. I was hustling during the day and rapping in the club at night. When they saw me doing my thing and making it happen, they just came to me and asked if I wanted to join them. I immediately said yes.

I wanted love and direction but I looked for those things in the wrong places. Often, young men and women join gangs because they are in need of guidance and love. Many of these young people were rejected in some way by their families. Whether the rejection came from family or society, these young people choose to belong to a group that will protect, love and guide them.

Most gang members do not know their biological fathers. Some of these young men were raised exclusively by their mothers or foster parents. Unfortunately, because of the rise of single parent homes, gangs have grown to phenomenal proportions in all cities and small towns. *"Be not deceived; bad company ruins good morals." – 1st Corinthians 15:33* These gangs breed corruption and destruction in whatever city, town, state or region they are in. Teachers and other leaders were surprised to know which students belong to gangs. Sometimes those who belong are quite obvious, while others are hiding in plain sight.

As a gang member, you are taught to hate. Often times, gang leaders order subordinates or those being initiated into the gang to kill a rival gang member on sight. It is an awful reality. As a gang member, I contributed to a lot destruction and violence in the streets.

My addictions were caused by perceived rejections and abuse. It didn't occur to me that it was my dad's loss. He was the one who rejected me. Behind the addictions, I lost out on countless things. In my latter years, my addictions were the reason for my relationships, both personal and professional, to crumble and be destroyed. Three of my marriages were destroyed due to one or more of my addictions. I have lost jobs and economic opportunities because of my addictions. There were times when I thought the addictions were gone, only to have people who I trusted to coax me and influence me to use again. That is why you have to be so careful about who you lay down with. Many people are so hell bent on their gratification; they will drag you down with them.

A word of wisdom to those who are using, want to stop using or have stopped using - do not fool yourself; if you are not careful, you can find yourself constantly relapsing, just to cope with the ups and downs of life. As you start to openly read the Word of God, the one thing you will NOT find is life is easy. It is not. I am living proof of that. Life is a constant uphill battle for a recovering addict, but with the Lord on your side, you can do anything you put your mind to.

It is important for me to emphasize how much of a role my addictions played in the earlier, unsaved years of my life. Even after I came to Christ, I relapsed back into drug use when things seemed hopeless. Like with my momma, I constantly relapsed while dealing with that whole piece. For me, drug use was often a coping mechanism for any problem I had. I disappeared for days at a time to binge on my drug of choice. I found myself in crack dens, gutters, drug parties in the projects, and dark corners of the clubs. I found myself in the bed of a strange woman I picked up at the club, or the corner. The instant gratification was what I thought I needed and wanted at the time. I used drugs, alcohol, sex and anger to get through countless situations in my life. I hustled, manipulated, lied, cheated, stole and beat down people to get what I wanted. I robbed people in the streets by gun point. The drugs, alcohol, sex, and anger were how I coped with poverty, lack and the daily drama of dealing with my momma's demons. It was only the grace of God that kept me from taking a life.

My father was not a part of my life at all. I barely knew Thomas Morrison because I had only seen him a few times. My primary role models were my mother, my sisters and the flurry of men that were in and out of my mother's life. Many times, I was taught by Momma's men to steal, cheat, and rob to survive on the streets. I still did not have good role models by the time I was a teenager. I was still acting out of perversion, lifting up women's and girl's dresses for a temporary thrill. I kept doing what I wanted to do. However, rapping was often a positive outlet for me to vent my frustrations about life. I was rapping and making up my own original lyrics and songs. I wrote a lot of rap songs about all of the things I went through on a daily basis.

I smoked a lot of cigarettes. I smoked whatever cigarette was available to me. I was a real smoker. I wasn't picky about cigarette brands at all. When you are nicking extremely bad, a cigarette is a cigarette, a loosie is a loosie. Momma sent me to the store a lot of times for her cigarettes, forty ounce of Old English and rolling papers. When she sent for a pack, I grabbed a pack for myself. When she was running low, she sent me to the store for a couple of loosies (cigarettes that were sold in quantities of 1 to 5). Remember, these were the days before you were carded. In those days, a five-year-old could walk into the nearest corner store and get a couple of cartons of cigarettes, a couple of forties and rolling papers if they said they were for their mother or father. That factor made getting cigarettes, beer and other alcohol I needed so much easier. I also used to sneak into the garage with my sisters and smoke whatever cigarettes they had.

It was during my teenage years when I started smoking weed heavily. My homies and I used to buy $5 joints from Mister Green (yes that was his real last name). Later on, I used to do cavies (cigarettes with cocaine in them). I started smoking my premos (weed and crack) later down the line. This combination took me through enormous problems. I started drinking whatever I could get my hands on. A lot of malt liquor could be gotten with just pocket change back in the day. Yes, there were times I used to do drugs and smoke weed with my momma, my stepfathers or the men who were in and out of my mom's life.

There were a lot of times in which my sisters and I stepped in to protect our mother from her men. Many of them used to act out in anger when they could not control her. They tried to jump on her with pushing or shoving. We often had to step in to keep these men from putting their hands on our momma. I took my anger out on these men for trying to hurt Momma. Some got the message quickly. Others took a few times of me using them for batting practice to get the point.

It was in my teenage years when I began a life of crime and I got involved with my true love…rap. I loved rapping about what I was going through at the time. Essentially, I was a very emotional teenager. I rapped about my momma, my sisters, my absent father, easy girls in the projects and growing up poor. I loved daydreaming about being rich and famous. I oftentimes fantasized about being in the limelight as a famous rapper. As a genre, rap started being authentically popular around my teenage years. This was before people started distinguishing between East Coast and West Coast artists. This was before battles and beefs were taken off wax (rappers fighting each other in real life rather than doing through a rap song diss). I listened to everybody back then. The Sugar Hill Gang, Kurtis Blow, Run DMC, Grand Master Flash, you name it. Rap music was my escape; it was my primary drug of choice. Rapping was what I did to chill and take my mind off of all the problems I had. Rapping made me feel good.

I received my first robbery conviction at the age of 14. There was a lot going on when I decided to rob people on the streets. The emotions which ran through me were voluminous. I started a life of crime because of desperation. Survival will make you creative and adventurous to the most mild mannered and meekest person. I felt myself turn into an angry heathen, hell bent on destruction and chaos. Throwing caution to the wind, I settled in for the quickest way to get money. I had to man-up and take control for my household. We had no food in the house.

I thought my mom was dying. She had come home from a wild drug binge with her people. She had been out of the house for a few days. She had done a lot of drugs. I knew she favored crack and Ritalin, but there was no telling what kind of drugs she had gotten a hold of. She came home and just crashed. She was passed out in bed for a couple of days. I shook her, but she did not respond. I was so scared she was going to die. I climbed into bed and went to sleep right beside her. I talked to her but she did not talk back to me at all. I was seriously scared and didn't know what to do. I felt so powerless. I had no father around to get me through this. One day, out of instinct, I just had enough of my mom being passed out. I undressed Momma. I used all of my strength and I dragged her to the tub. I ran water over her. She came to. At first, she was resistant. "NO!" she exclaimed in protest. "Stop it. I want to sleep." She was mad and started cursing at me, but I didn't care. As the water ran on her in the tub, she slowly started to wake up. I dried her off, put her robe on her, and put her back in bed. I was so relieved she was awake. I sat in the chair in front of her bed and just looked at her. After a few minutes, she sat up in the bed by herself. She was still kind of out of it. She was holding her head. It was as if she was resurrected from the dead. I will never forget what she told me next. She said,

"One day, it's not going to be like this. One day you are going to be somebody. I hope you never stop rapping and singing because that's what's going to bring you success in your life. You sing very well; you rap really well and you make your own songs up. You are going to go extremely far in your life. You are going to be very successful." Momma essentially knew how to make me feel good and to put things into perspective, when things were chaotic. Even after she woke up, we were still in a desperate situation. There was still no food or money in the house.

During this time, I was hanging out and running the streets with this guy named Milo. He was a real cool dude. He ran with gangbangers much of the time. He had a very bad influence on me, but I genuinely liked him. I could talk to him about a lot of things that were going on. Unlike other people my age, he could actually sympathize with what I was going through. The day before, I told him about the situation at home. He had pity on me and wanted to help out in any way he could. Milo already had a long rap sheet. He was well acquainted with the juvenile justice system. He did his first lick (robbery) at the age of 11. He was an opportunist. Milo was all about getting quick money by any means necessary. He saw a problem as an opportunity to break the law. He was used to breaking the law. He robbed, stole, and cheated to get the things he needed to survive. The next day, after I told him about the drama going on at the house, he met me on the stoop of the emergency shelter that my Momma, my sister and I were staying at.

He showed me this gun. It was a snub nose .38 that he stole it from his father. Milo said, "Look, this is my dad's gun. Let's take it and go make some money." I wasn't as brave as he. After all, this was my first robbery. He said, "Relax. There's nothing to it. You never have to pull the trigger. No one ever gets hurt. It is not that big of a deal. I rob people all of the time. I kept money." He kind of put my mind at ease, but I needed a little more encouragement to start making money. I needed to man up at this point and do what needed to be done. So, Milo and I went to the store and got a couple of 40 ounces of malt liquor for ourselves. *(this was way before they carded people)* I needed some liquid courage to do my first robbery.

Growing up, I used to see guns but never held one myself. I was a bit scared of guns. I never had to resort to sticking up people just to survive, until now. After Milo and I got the 40 ounces, we sat on the steps in the back of the building and got twisted. Little did I know this was the gateway to a pattern of bad behavior. I got my liquid or burnt courage drunk to steal, cheat, or rob to get what I needed. After Milo and I drank our 40 ounces of Old English, I was ready to go and get that paper.

We walked down Madison Street. I was nervous at first. On the first mark (you never see them as victims until the cops classify them as such), my hand was shaky. I was so nervous until I probably scared them more than anything else. I followed Milo's lead and we robbed people left and right. As we robbed more and more people, I got the hang of it. From one person I got $26. I surely didn't see them as victims. I saw the people I robbed as a means to an end. We stopped after a while and celebrated. We got some food and just hung around the block.

It was fun while it lasted, but I soon learned there were going to be consequences for our actions. An hour later, the police was looking for us. We ducked into a mini mart. There were three police cars searching for us.

I looked at Milo and said, "Hey we got to split up, Milo. We have a better chance of dodging the cops that way. We also have to get rid of this gun."

Milo said, "Cool, I will see you when I see you." So, we split up. Instead of being on the main street, I took to the back alleys, trying to escape from the cops but they finally caught up with me. I tried to throw my gun. I ran, but I could not get away from them. The cops blocked me off three different ways. They took me. They searched and found the gun I committed the robberies with.

They said, "Yep, this is one of our robbers. Where is your partner?"

I said, "I don't know anything about a partner and I surely don't know anything about a robbery. You got the wrong guy." No matter what I told them, they were not buying it.

One of the officers then asked me, "How old are you son?"

I said, "I am thirteen years old."

The officer said, "Well, son, you have just made it to the big leagues, put your hands behind your back." That day, the police charged me with four counts of armed robbery with a handgun. To this day, I can't carry a firearm.

They sent me to the state department of corrections. They locked me up in a juvenile detention center before they sentenced me. I met people like me who were going through lots of drama at home. Many guys who were there didn't know their father either. The ones who did know their father said they barely knew the guy. Many were the sons of single mothers who were alcoholics and drug addicts. Ironically, I learned more about crime and how to commit crime while on the inside. I was there for an entire year. After one year, they sentenced me to 129 weeks (2 years and 5 ½ months) in juvenile prison. I received no credit for time served.

There were moments when I wanted to desperately get out and go check my momma and the rest of my family. However, there were other times when I felt a sense of relief to be off the streets and away from the drama. No, I wasn't on a vacation, but I was eating three meals per day. I was sleeping well, without hearing the screams of Momma or being disturbed by the footsteps of the multiple men Momma brought into our house or shelter. There was a part of me actually found comfort in being locked away, which turned out not to be good (when you actually get comfortable in prison, you gain a tolerance to commit crime because you don't mind doing the time). I met many young men in juvenile detention with the same sentiment. Some dreaded the thought of being released to go back home and into a rough situation. After being locked up all those years and months, my custody level went down, but I was still legally in prison. They sent me to a group home in the upstate.

The group home setting was supposed to help me to adjust back to certain freedoms and prepare me to re-enter civilization outside. While in the group home, I was required to attend high school, I was a freshman.

The group home counselor took us to school. I tried out and got on the football team. While I was playing football, I got into very good shape. I was working out, doing drills at practice and doing a lot of running. I was also eating right. I managed to find pleasure and enjoyment while being at the home. The willing girls at school and football games made me feel like a normal teenager, but it was short lived. I was soon released to go home so

I had to stop playing football.

I started to get kind of bummed out over the fact that my group home stage was over. I had to return to the city, but I made good use of the time. I enjoyed *playing football* and having a small sense of normalcy, while it lasted. The only thing I looked forward to, at that point, was seeing Momma.

As my stay in the group home was nearing its end, Thomas Morrison, Sr., the man who I thought was my father, passed away. My counselor from the group home took me to the funeral. Although I was in the group home, I was still in the custody of the State Department of Corrections (DOC). Legally, I still had to go to his funeral in shackles and hand cuffs. I surely didn't like doing it, but it was the protocol, since I was still the property of the State DOC. At the burial, the counselor permitted me to go up to the grave. It felt like I was looking at the grave of a perfect stranger.

I looked inside and told my counselor, "Man, I don't know this dude. I met this guy once or twice in my life. Man, I don't want to stay here, I am ready to go. I don't know this person."

The counselor said, "It doesn't bother you that he's gone?"

I said, "No, it doesn't bother me because I don't even know this person. I am ready to go." So, we went back to the group home.

Those last months in the group home flew by. My release day finally came. My momma came to the home and picked me up. When I saw her, I hugged her tight, I was so glad to see her. The day she came to get me from the group home was one of the happiest days of my life.

THE EVERYDAY HUSTLE
Chapter Five

I started hustling as a drug dealer at a very young age. When you start hustling as a drug dealer, the money usually looks good at first, then, reality sets in. The money never seems to be enough in the long run. Hustling also has some heavy costs, if you are not careful. I went through a lot when I first got started.

As I settled back into my routine at home, things got back to normal. Our family's normal included smoking, shooting up and dealing dope. Through it all, my momma and I were indeed close. While my sisters were doing their own thing, Momma and I were hustling. We often hustled in the dope house and we were packing with a .22 or .38. yes, if you saw my momma in a dope house, you saw me, sitting very close, chilling and protecting my momma.

When I was in jail and got out, I did not have to worry about anything because Momma paid all of my bills, cooked my food, and kept some of the dealers off me when I didn't do right. Although I drove a lot, I didn't have a driver's license (*I racked up a bunch of tickets because of it*). At night, I climbed in bed with Momma and went to sleep right next to her. Momma was a good person. She had a kind heart even with her issues.

I had opportunities to hang out with my sisters at the club. My sisters were also bona fide hustlers. They came packing heat with them. They needed protection while on the streets of the city.

On one such occasion, of my sisters and I went to this club. The club was jumping that night. There were other hustlers in the building; chilling. My sister and I were having fun. This guy whom neither of us knew approached us. He must have seen us take out money for drinks.

He said to my sister, "Let me have five dollars."

My sis said, "No, I don't have five dollars."

He asked again, "Let me have five dollars."

My sis said, "I don't know you."

He said, "You don't have to know me, just give me five dollars."

My sister said, "I said no."

The guy got bold and called my sister the –b- word and cursed her out (my sister hates to be called the –b- word).

My sister got loud with him and cursed him out. She then opened her coat to show the man she was packing and said, "Do we have a problem? DO WE HAVE A PROBLEM?" He walked away, very quickly and quietly. Then the cops were called so we got out of there quick, fast and in a hurry.

As an aspiring hustler, I was doing my best to find my way in the world. Often times, this meant going to different states and learning different angles of the game. When I started slinging drugs, I did my best not to use drugs at all. I learned doing your own product causes many problems. I did smoke a little weed from time to time (if you know street credo, you know weed is not considered a hard drug). However, I didn't touch cocaine or crack. I sold nickel and dime bags.

Over time, I became bolder and better. I stood on the corner with a 9mm in my waistband, in case someone thought to rob me or try to challenge me for my corner. I was not to be played with and anybody who knew me from former times would vouch for that. I have been known to shoot at those who tried to play me. I scared people to keep them at bay so they wouldn't mess with me. In the streets, some corners are sacred because they were prime real estate, and that was because of the traffic. Some drug addicts frequented certain corners over others. When you are in the drug game, you actually have to be on your guard against the competition. The streets are vicious. If someone indeed wanted your corner, you could be shot or killed, just to be lord over a street corner.

When I was dealing, it appeared I could never make enough money. It burned through my hands as fast as I could make it. Due to my drug habits, I had to stay on the grind, looking for my next hustle or score.

To say the least, my life was unstable in *every* sense of the word. I felt I was the poster child for a *degenerate*. I was a reprobate and was at the time powerless to do anything about it. The streets had my mind enslaved and there was no freedom in my mind, my soul, my will, my spirit, my intellect, or my imagination; I'm telling you NOWHERE! I couldn't see it nor could I smell it. All my sensory were completely dull. I allowed my conscience to die. I was a felon with many strikes against me. I am not just talking law strikes, but life strikes. When you live life constantly trying to hustle and survive, it is truly tough.

One of my sisters got a money green Cadillac. She got the money for it by walking the hoe stroll (prostitution). She didn't need a pimp to make money either. She made sure to stay street smart and savvy. She made some good money on the streets by not having to answer to a greedy pimp. These were the days you didn't have to have a driver's license or car insurance to buy a car. I was so jealous and proud of her at the same time. I wanted a money green Caddy just like her. My sister had discovered the everyday hustle she could lean on for her survival. She knew how to handle her johns and keep it moving. Her having that Caddy was one of my motivations for hustling and dealing dope. Of course, survival was another motivation, but that Caddy was something to behold, white leather seats, wood grain interior and white wall tires.

When you are in spiritual bondage, often times, the physical and tangible things uplift you most. The sight of that beautiful Caddy motivated me to step up my selling and dealing, but I needed to get a good hustle going to get a caddy just like my sister's. My sister tried to be my mentor and help me get into the pimping game. Other men in our family managed to do it and they were successful.

My sister actually came through for me one day. She brought this girl home for me to pimp out. It didn't go as planned. Yes, she had the looks, and her body was banging. I could have gotten some mileage out of her on the hoe stroll, but it wasn't meant to be. Like all respectful pimps, I had to take her for a test drive before I put her on the road. She had an STD (sexually transmitted disease). Shamefully, I caught the clap from her when I took her for a test drive. We then parted ways. That business relationship wouldn't have worked out. For an aspiring pimp, a diseased prostitute is very bad for business. I was so disappointed because I still wanted to get a money green Caddy just like my sister's.

I became ambitious. I started dealing drugs so I could get myself a Caddy. Momma's dealings with all of those gangbangers, drug lords and kingpins helped me out greatly. I didn't have to look far for advice or merchandise. They provided insight, advice, distribution, and guidance. I was able to get a lot of drugs and dope to sell. They showed me how to cook the crack and break it down into crack rocks. They showed me how to break the weed I got down into nickels, dimes, quarters, ounces and pounds. I dealt cocaine, and a lot of crack. I had some pills such as Ritalin to shoot up. To shoot up Ritalin, you'd get a pill or two and dissolve it in water. Unfortunately, Ritalin was my mom's drug of choice. After months of slinging (dealing drugs) and hustling on the streets, I was making bank. I finally got a money green Cadillac of my own and she was beautiful. I didn't have a driver's license but I didn't care. I had gotten my Caddy and soon, I followed up with the purchase of a blue Riviera.

Sometimes, I dealt drugs out of my girls' apartment (who ever I was sleeping with at the time). In my early 20's, my momma was a known drug mule for gangbangers, kingpins and drug lords in surrounding cities. She drove to and through several cities and did drug pickups. Sometimes, I went with her. She got very creative in hiding all of the drugs and contraband in her car.

Gangbanging started to slowly fade away as life became more about the hustle for me.

The hustle took me to different cities. There were women galore. As I kept slinging and dealing, the money looked great. I came up with a better strategy. In my drug dealing, I used to skimp off the top of the bag. I did this much of the time with weed and cocaine, especially when I sold anything more than an eight ball (1/8 of an ounce of cocaine). There were times I came up so short on my distributor's cash, they sent their boys after me. Many times, they beat me up to straighten me out. My momma stepped in many times on my behalf. Her ties ran deep with some of these kingpins and drug lords. She saved me time and time again from being hurt or fatally wounded.

In one particular city, I did a burglary with this dude. Things went bad and we wound up going to jail for a year. Inside the jail, I met this girl who worked in the kitchen, we got particularly close.

After I was released, she was waiting outside for me. I stayed with her for a few weeks. I thought we were getting serious but it didn't work out. I had to leave her house because I could not find a job. This made me homeless but I had connections. I ended up staying in a crack house. As thanks for letting me stay in the house, I often provided them crack and cocaine and I brought groceries from time to time.

I met these older guys who rapped and hustled. These guys had it going on. I drove around with them for a couple of days. They sold a lot of drugs. They were concerned about me staying in the crack house. They said I needed to get out of there because anything could happen.

One said, "There have been shoot outs in that alley. We don't want to see you get hurt in there." So they set me up in their house. It was just a house where customers came to purchase dope and leave. They assured me it was safe. Another guy and I ran the house. Every day they kept us fully loaded with a pistol and dope. I ended up sitting there all day, selling dope, watching TV, and writing my music.

There was this crack fiend who I used to send to buy me weed sacks. One day we started smoking this joint and all of a sudden, I started feeling intuitively funny. The joint smelled funny so I asked her what was in it. She said she laced it up with some crack. Back home, those were premos. I was hooked. I liked the feeling it gave me but that was not good. It's bad to get hooked on your own product. After I smoked that, I ended up smoking up half my profit.

The very next week, the guy who ran the house ended up giving me a bigger sack. I smoked it all, with the help of the people across the street in the crack house. They swore to help me get the money back. They left me hanging. I only had $100 ($200 short). The guy assured me it was cool. A little bit later, two of his boys come through. All of a sudden, the guy said come here for a moment, I want to show you something. Before I knew it, these guys were beating me down. They must have wailed on me for a few seconds. They busted my nose.

COPING IN THE DOPE GAME
Chapter Six

One day, everything in my life changed. I found myself at a crossroad. When you are busy dealing with demons plaguing your life, the crossroads of life are inevitable. You come to your crossroads when you are at your breaking point. The streets, the stealing, the drug dealing, the drug addiction and the overall dysfunction was the life I came to know. It was my normal. When I started to change and want better for my life, I learned about destiny and how the devil can distract you from your purpose by enticing you through temptation. The devil does not tempt you with things you do not want. He tempts you with those things that excite you and give you instant (but temporary) gratification. For me, it was fast women, fast money, and other fast thrills.

By seeking the Lord diligently, I became aware of my purpose. As I became more aware of my purpose, I noticed my behavior patterns and how they distracted me from my true purpose. The devil comes to kill, steal and destroy, but Christ came that we may have the abundant life.

After everything I went through, I still loved my family. My family wasn't exactly stable and they weren't living right either. Despite my constant objections, my mother was a drug mule for gang members. Often times she risked her freedom and her life for people who could care less about her well-being.

Although my mother had many problems, she was my

stability. By my early 20's, I could not cook. I had never paid a bill. I didn't have a driver's license. She was one of the main means of my survival.

My breaking point happened in 1998. I found myself in a prison cell after I caught a case for selling to an undercover cop. I remembered being worried about my momma. She was so good at coming to visit me while I was on the inside. She visited me at least once a week. When she didn't visit, I expected a call at least, but it had been a few days since I had heard anything from her. I figured maybe something came up.

It was about 3:10 am and it was very quiet, almost too quiet on the cell block. Despite the peace, for some reason, I couldn't sleep. I felt very uneasy. All of a sudden, my electronic cell block door opened. For a good five minutes, there was silence. I was lying in bed thinking the cell doors malfunctioned, but it was only my cell door that opened. Then I heard a guard say over the intercom, Prisoner 61999, step out and report to the cafeteria. So I got out of bed. I walked out of my cell. I went towards the cafeteria. I knew then, something was terribly wrong. Little did I know I was about to experience the worst day of my life.

As I started walking it was very dark. All I could see was a small shiny cross. As I got closer, I perceived it was the chaplain and a guard. The chaplain said, "I am so sorry son. Your family called us a few minutes ago. Your mom passed away this evening." As the chaplain talked, I felt overwhelming shock, disbelief, and grief.

I asked, "Are you serious?"

The chaplain repeated his words of consolation, "I'm sorry

for your loss. He said a short prayer for me. Through my tears, I said, thank you and walked back to my cell. I was no good after that. I went to bed but couldn't sleep. I was overcome with emotion; knowing I would never see her again. I got up and I started writing music. I wrote gospel music and dedicated it to my momma.

My momma died alone and without me. I cried out loud in my prison cell. I was crying and crying, praying and praying for God to take the pain away. The pain was so very deep and heavy on me. I asked Him to just to take the breath and life out of me. I just wanted to be with my mom. I felt like I didn't have anyone. I was beyond devastation and depression.

In the days to follow, I didn't want to go to the yard. I did not want to talk to anyone. The homies on the block saw I wasn't coming out my cell. I was crying all of the time. They found out through the commanding officer what happened. They showed me so much love. They sent me care packages from the commissary, and they sent notes and cards. Many gave condolences and shout outs as they passed by my cell. One said, "The homies love you and are so sorry for your loss. Let us know if you need anything." I cried for days. *"The eyes of the Lord are on the righteous and his ears are attentive to their cry." – **Psalms 34:15*** Despite all of the problems and all of the drama I witnessed over the years, I still missed her terribly.

I later discovered she had a lung infection. All I knew was I had to see her one last time to say goodbye and to get some kind of closure. The warden allowed me to go to the funeral. But I had to go to her funeral in shackles and chains and accompanied by armed correction officers. I also had to pay $2800 for the guard detail. One of my partners in the music business gladly fit the bill for me to go to the funeral. The funeral was in a church. The church was packed. It was standing room only. Although my mother stayed in trouble for much of her life, she had a lot of people who cared and loved her. Lots of her gangster associates and baby fathers showed up. My sisters were there with their children. My aunts, uncles and cousins were there. There were family members in the church I had not seen in decades. I came into the funeral in my prison suit. While all eyes were on me, I shuffled my way down the church center aisle. I had two officers who had to stay with me the entire time. I made my way down to her casket. When I got to the casket and saw my momma lying there dead, I completely lost it. I burst out crying Momma, Momma, Momma. My family sobbed loudly. I felt like I was about to have a nervous breakdown. I had to be restrained, taken to the prison infirmary and sedated. I nearly lost my mind that day. I was a mess. My family and I could not embrace each other. I never felt so alone.

    I don't care what type of relationship you have with your momma, if you live long enough for that inevitable time, seeing your mom in a casket will break you down. It was a heart-breaking scene. I am blessed I was able to recover from that in my right mind. I don't care what your mom does to you. I don't care what type of person your mom is or was, you will still love her. You still have that spot inside your heart for your mom. After all, she birthed you. She was the very first female you had involvement with.

    The worst part was I was in prison, unable to truly mourn my mom's death like I needed to. For several days, I was no good to anyone. I became a ticking time bomb. I told the commanding officer if I wasn't put in solitary confinement, I'd truly hurt somebody. They obliged and took me to confinement.

While in confinement, I mourned heavily. As I went through the process, I wrote music dedicating them to my momma, and prayed, asking God question after question. My momma was on various kinds of drugs. She went on binges and was often on the brink of overdosing. After all the drugs, I wondered why God took her. Why did she have to die while I was in prison? I did not understand why God took my momma at *this* stage in my life.

After my momma's death, life was never the same. Her death caused me to examine my life. It got to the point where writing rap lyrics about the streets no longer satisfied the endless hunger and thirst inside my spirit and soul. I got tired of continuously searching for something I could not explain. I needed my spirit man to be satisfied and fed. I thought the answer was to get out of jail, get more sex, drugs, money, and write more hip-hop music. However, I had to come to the realization these things were just temporary thrills. Sex, drugs, money and music can only take you so far. I mean, sure, these things will satisfy you for a short time, but when you reach the point where these things no longer satisfy you, it is time to search for something deeper.

Seeing my momma in that casket did something to me. It changed me forever. Her death woke me up. It was as if I had been on a 20 plus year binge of drugs, sex, music, alcohol, and prison life. Then, all of a sudden, I woke up from the dream. Like the prodigal son in **(Luke 15)**, I came to my senses.

The prodigal son was someone else in the Bible I could relate to. There was a rich man with two sons. One of the sons asked his father for his portion of the inheritance. The young man went and spent all of his money partying and living large.

When the money was gone, he found himself in the mud, with the pigs, actually considering eating the same pods the pigs were eating. This was the point in which he came to his senses. He swallowed his pride and went home, expected his father to be mad. However, the father celebrated the return of his son.

In order to be delivered from my past, I had to start looking towards the hills from which cometh my help *(Psalm 121:1)*. I started asking the hard questions, who am I? Why am I here on earth? Why didn't the suicides work? What is my true purpose? Why did I go through all of the things I went through and still make it out alive? Where did I go wrong? Do I want to die young like my momma? Who is my true soul mate, my help meet, the one who God has made for me? Where is the one who will love me for the man I am? What is the meaning of it all? I desired a woman who could truly be mine, but I couldn't find her.

When I started asking God all of these things, my life took a paradigm shift. A paradigm shift occurs when everything you knew as normal becomes foreign. I thank God my shift was a good shift. I had to look at my life to see how to change for the better. I had to ask myself if there was anything good, I could salvage from my life. I had to look way back to before everything in my life went downhill. I had to look at how life was, when I was a little boy.

When I was younger, I lived with my maternal grandparents and they were strict but, loving. They gave me a true sense of structure. They were early risers and early to bed. They literally got up with the chickens. When I was a young boy, one of the lessons my grandparents taught me was about the love God had for mankind. They took me to Sunday school and to church. My grandparents had me baptized when I was young. They taught me about how God gave His only begotten son Jesus, who was without sin, to take on the sins of mankind. They taught me about how He died on the cross for our sins and redeemed us.

I was a good little boy, but when I went to live with my mom full-time, those teachings disappeared. Since she was mostly in the streets, I trained myself to survive. The hard-core streets became my nurturer at an early age. I looked to what I knew and got my lessons on stealing and dope dealing. The gang banging soon followed, along with the pimping, the drug addictions and the constant prison sentences. I strayed away from all of the things my grandparents taught me as a little boy.

When I was a child, I did not fully understand why Jesus died for me, but when I was in prison, I had nothing but time to learn new things. I had time to think. In prison, you have to make some hard decisions which can either make you or break you. You can either use the time to network with your fellow inmates in order to learn how to become a better criminal and commit more crimes when you get out, or you can use the time to better yourself. When you want change to truly take place in your life, your actions and thoughts have to change. You have to pursue better things. Remember, if nothing changes, then nothing changes! Profound.

I used my time to learn more about Christ Jesus. I had time to pray, seek His face and truly read and study the Word of God for myself. It is great to have people teach you about Jesus and the Word of God, but there is nothing like learning about Jesus and the Word of God for yourself. I took advantage of the prison time to build my faith and actively pursue Jesus. As an adult, I was grateful and humbled when I learned about Jesus for myself. It takes maturity to get into the deeper matters of God.

⌘(FOCUS SCRIPTURE)⌘

God is close to the brokenhearted **Psalm 34:18**
Our souls waited for the Lord He is our help and our Shield. **Psalms 33: 20**
So that your faith might not rest on human wisdom but God's power.
1 Corinthians 2:5

RUNNING FROM THE GAME
Chapter Seven

I started dealing drugs with one of my babies' mommas (before she became my baby momma). We shall call her Liz. First, it was just business between us. Liz was a bona fide hustler. She was extremely deep in the game when we met. She had already made a name for herself in the game when I hooked up with her. She was already good by herself, but when we got together, it was something to behold. We became attracted to each other and we got into a serious relationship. We dealt so much dope together; it wasn't funny. We sold a lot of weight in coke and weed. The money was looking awesome, but it didn't last long. Fast money doesn't last long you know. *"Dishonest money dwindles away, but whoever gathers money little by little makes it grow." –* **Proverbs 13:11**

The faster you get it, the faster you lose it. As time went by, things started falling apart. Someone snitched on us. The FEDS kicked our door in. They searched and tossed the apartment until we could not recognize it, but it was cool. No matter how hard they searched, they never found our stash. I had already sold everything we had. I hustled all night to get rid of our inventory. Rather than wait for the FEDS to come back to the apartment, Liz and I decided to leave the state. We left an apartment full of furniture. By the time the FEDS came back, we were several states away. They came and took everything in the apartment. We didn't care. It was just me and her. We had to run, and we didn't tell anyone where we were going.

When we got to the next city, we laid low. Although this was a big city, we took no chances. I got two jobs so I could support us both. Liz didn't ask me for much. There was one thing she wanted more than anything—a child of her own. It wasn't as if we didn't try. We were dedicated to putting in the work. After a time, I knew it wasn't me.

In the city, we found a place which was very reasonable. We stayed in this building above a church. We attended church services all the time. It was life changing. I sensed the Holy Ghost was in the building. They didn't sugar coat things. I didn't sell any drugs while in the apartment. I felt like the entire building was blessed. While we were living there, a miracle happened. Liz conceived her first child. We were so happy, or so I thought.

One day, I went to work at one of my jobs and I missed her while at work. I couldn't wait to get home to see her. When I went upstairs, it was almost too quiet. When I opened the door, I called her. No answer. I went to the closet, her clothes were gone, but mine were still there. I thought Liz was happy being there with me. Deep down, she was scared. It was her first child and she wanted to be with her family. She left a note which said, "*I love you but I don't want to be here anymore. I have what I wanted from you. I want to be around my family while I have this child. If you want to be with me, you have to come back.*" I was very hesitant. I didn't want to go back. I was taking a huge chance by going back, but I loved her and our unborn child so I had to go back. I waited a couple of days then I decided I needed to see about her. I drove for several hours to get back home. When I finally got to their house, her mother and sister told me where she was. When I found her, I found her with another man. I was furious. I slapped her and walked off. From that point on, she had a restraining order on me and I could not see my daughter. After that, I relapsed again into heavy cocaine use, to deal with that pain.

FOCUS SCRIPTURE

These six things the Lord hates; Indeed, seven are repulsive to Him: A proud look [the attitude that makes one overestimate oneself and discount others], a lying tongue, And hands that shed innocent blood, A heart that creates wicked plans, Feet that run swiftly to evil, A false witness who breathes out lies [even half-truths], And one who spreads discord (rumors) among brothers.
Proverbs 6:16-19 (AMP)

THE RAP GAME
Chapter Eight

I give God all of the glory for the transformation that has taken place in me. I thank God I am a brand-new creature in Christ and old things have passed away. Transformation is a process; it wasn't an overnight thing. I had to pray my way through and uniformly now, I have to plead the blood of Jesus over situations I face.

My earlier struggle in the secular rap game prepared me for the success I now enjoy in the gospel rap industry today. I learned how to navigate channels and get my music heard back in the day. As I mentioned before, rapping was my positive outlet. Despite all of the dysfunction and chaos I called life, my creative side was alive and blazing. Although I was caught up into drug dealing, alcohol and women, the hunger for music kept me alive and focused.

I had a lot of influences from the music world and I didn't discriminate. It didn't matter if it was East Coast rap or West Coast rap, I listened to some of everybody. I listened to artists like Grand Master Flash, Heavy D, Kool Moe Dee, LL Cool J, and Eric B to name a few. I also listened to a lot of rhythm and blues, and pop. Stars like Michael Jackson, Chaka Khan, and Teddy Pendergrass were in my cassette player. During all of the turmoil, one of the small pleasures my sisters and I had was music. We pretended we were music groups in concert. We used mops, brooms and other things as microphones.

If you were a rap artist back in the day, you could not go about it alone. In today's times because of social media and different music apps, you can enter the rap game all by your lonesome and still be successful. Back in the day, I was privileged to have music partners.

I partnered with this dude in my neighborhood, we will call him Tim. He was a great partner to me. He helped me make my mix tapes. Tim and I often sold the mix tapes out the trunk. We went out during the height of the day, stood on the corner, and peddled the mixtapes. That is how rap music was often distributed back then. It was hard to get a record played on the radio if you were an unknown or had a lot of cursing on the record.

Most of the time when audiences hear a rap artist, they are listening to the final product. A lot of work goes into that final product. Take lyrics for instance, you need to have a good flow and you need lyrics relevant to your audience. If your listening base is in the inner city, they certainly do not want to hear about life in the suburbs. Secular Rap audiences want to hear about what they are experiencing or want to experience. The secular rap and hip-hop audiences want to hear lyrics about making money by any means, the life of drug dealers, about smoking weed, sexual conquests and about living.

Rap music was my true love. It fulfilled me because I could escape from all the drama and turmoil in my life. It was most often the pad and pen that held me through some crucial times. I loved writing and performing my original rap music. Talking about the street life was usually the theme of my performances. You could say I was testifying about my life as a hustler, pimp, gang banger, dope dealer, and being arrested.

The rap game is not for the faint at heart. There are many

great rap artists you have never heard of and will never hear of, simply because they gave up. An abundance of aspiring rap artists think they can just belt out a few lyrics, get their demo out, instantly get signed to a label and get rich in a matter of moments. It does not happen like that. When fame and fortune don't instantly show up, many aspiring rap artists quit and give up on their dreams. Let's get it straight, I had to work hard; plain and simple!

There were three keys for staying in the rap game back then. First, you had to make sure you stayed busy forging relationships with like-minded artists. Second, networking with others in the music business (DJ's, producers, promoters), and third, perseverance. If you were able to do these three and if you had dedicated partners by your side, you at least had a fighting chance.

Through it all, I was still an aspiring rapper. When I wasn't hustling, I rapped in various rap contests and won. I astounded the judges with the way I flowed. My lyrics were tight. I did a lot of freestyle. After all, I lived and breathed rap. My whole lifestyle, at that time, was the essence of hip hop; starting out at the bottom and rising to the top.

After a while, the opportunity to join the ranks of the soldiers of rap had come. One night, after I had won a contest at a club, a famous rap producer approached me. He told me I was awesome and I was just the sound they were looking for at his record label. I had to drive across several states to get to him. I was so excited. Only a few cats catch breaks and score recording deals in this game. I hustled so my gear was tight when I walked into the record company. The day came. When I walked into the studio of the record company, I remember the feeling of excitement showering me. I was so excited to be there. As I walked through the hallways, I passed many familiar faces I enjoyed listening to on the radio waves. I got the chance to talk to a couple of them. As I continued to walk through the halls, I saw platinum records on the walls. I shook hands with the producers and I remember feeling both excited and hesitant at the same time. Something didn't feel right. I had heard some good things and some bad things about the record producer, but I fought off my feelings and started to perform. This was my chance. When I got into the recording both, I just killed it. I laid down those lyrics. As I performed, I was in the zone. It felt so natural for me to be in the studio performing. After I was finished, I was overjoyed.

The producers had heard enough. They were ready for me to sign the contract and join the ranks of the rappers who fueled the Hip Hop era. They gave me the contract to have my lawyer to look over. They were going to give me a $75,000 signing bonus. Liz and I took the contract and left for home. As we left the building, I had a funny feeling, but I shook it off, got into the car and headed home to find a lawyer to go over the contract with me. This contract was my chance to leave the hustle for good. Instead, greed cost me greatly and I lost the chance of a lifetime.

THE CROSSROADS: THE DAY EVERYTHING CHANGED
Chapter Nine

I was still in the world, but I desperately needed to change in order to be truly transformed into the Sanktifed Soulja which God called me to be. I was dealing with a lot of rejection; rejection from my father and from the women who I thought loved me. However, with the women, I felt I caused some of the rejection on myself because I could not control the drug addiction and my anger. Demons are REAL! I wanted to get away from the drugs and gangbanging. My soul was constantly crying out. I was in a relentless search for true love.

The quickest way to relieve my loneliness was lust and the quickest relief for my frustrations was anger. I struggled so much with lust and anger.

Prison can often be a refuge for the criminal. It is a place where the criminal can regroup. It is also a brutal place where I have seen men become victims. One of the worst things you could ever hear while you are in a jail cell is the sound of a man yelling for help. Then you hear the man getting hit, then silence. Then the one raping the man says, "Next." It is a brutal place, yet millions of men find themselves behind bars every day.

Prison does offer some positive options. I worked out, got an education and went to anger management classes to get help. In prison I took advantage of every opportunity. I was on work crews. I worked in the kitchen so I ate well. I read a lot of books and I stayed involved. Although I made a lot of enemies on the outside because of my gang ties, it was different for me on the inside. I kept my nose clean. Much of the time, I stayed to myself. I had to do that. Although I made friends with people on the inside, I knew the best means of coping was to stay to myself.

There were plenty of fellas on the inside who were frequent flyers. These were the guys who kept coming back to jail, and sometimes on purpose. They often refer to prison as three hots and a cot (three hot meals and a cot to sleep on).

When you see people who become either dependent or tolerant of being in prison, they are often chronically homeless. Oftentimes, because they are dependent on the kindness of others for a place to stay, they find themselves going in and out of the walls of the prison system when all else fails. It is unfortunate there are many men and women who resort to this lifestyle. However, many find themselves unable to come out of this endless cycle. Many laws have to change, but in the meantime, people must move in faith in order to break the cycle. I used prison as a means of survival when I ran out of options, and especially when I was homeless on the streets.

It was hard for me to trust anyone. I often let my guard down at the wrong time. I still associated with people who wanted to trick me, especially women. The hustler got hustled. I still didn't have that transformed mind. I was still in the world. I still reacted with violence when it was time to act with a level head. I needed to change in order to be truly transformed into the Sanktified Soulja which God called me to be. I was not perfect back then and I am not perfect now, but I strive to be better today than I was yesterday.

Whenever I was on the inside, it was like I was dead to the world. Girlfriends and wives didn't take the time to come and visit. My babies' mothers never consider letting my babies come to see me. My boys did not bother to call or write. When I was on the inside, I stayed to myself, but sometimes that did not work. I am a big guy and I lifted weights to add muscle to the meat. Subsequently, there was an occasional idiot who tried me. There is an old tale in the jail systems that if you get in jail and you want to seem tough and assert power, you have to beat up the biggest guy on the yard. At one point, I was the biggest guy on the yard and a little runt of a man decided to try me. On one such occasion, I was walking the yard and this guy walked up on me acting crazy. I guess he had heard the myth, became froggy, and tried to jump. He was yelling at me. I beat that boy down so bad; I nearly caught a case for murder. As a matter of fact, while I was wailing on him, an officer in the watch tower shot down, right near my feet. He shouted, "Get down on the ground." I did as instructed, but when the officers came to get me, they restrained me and put me in solitary confinement.

When I was in jail, the correction officers liked to provoke the inmates for extra time in solitary confinement. They taunted folks until they acted. Being in jail was hard enough, but solitary confinement was something else. Solitary confinement is designed to break the human spirit. It made even the hardest criminal break down and cry.

I stayed in solitary confinement for a while because I threw my food tray at the officers. Afterwards, I cooled down. I started getting more privileges and that made life a little more bearable on the inside.

Just think about this: you're sitting in jail because your baby's mama turned you in for not paying child support, or you beat up somebody in a fit of rage. You're in and out of relationships like a revolving door, and you keep running from your responsibilities. That's not the way to live. You have to help that woman you made babies with. This is a huge problem in our society. We must correct these insatiable desires and appetites to sin. These habits will turn into curses and go throughout our generations.

The babies being made did not ask to be born. It is time out from placing the blame on others. You need to start taking full responsibility for your actions. We have to move forward. Yes, that means getting out of the gangbanging, stop slinging and selling dope to make a living and go actually train for a new job.

I have found most cats in jail are sitting on hidden talents. Many of them were a force to be reckoned with in the streets because they tried to outsell every drug dealer on the block. Just imagine if you actually got out and went legit, without guns, violence or intimidation? What if they actually took the skills they learned on the streets and made great use of them, tapping into talent that could cause positive changes in our lives? In jail, it can start by making realistic goals. For me, changes started happening when I started to distance myself from the rest of the cliques in prison. I tried to stay to myself most of the time, because I didn't want any more trouble. There was something within me driving me to think differently.

One year when I was in prison, I was blessed to share a cell with an older man. He was in for drug distribution. He was one of the kindest and wisest people I've ever met. *"Listen to advice and accept instruction, that you may gain wisdom in the future. Many are the plans in the mind of the man. But it is the purpose of the Lord that will stand."* **Proverbs**

19:20-21 When God gets ready to prepare you for kingdom work, He will surround you with wise council.

This man taught me a lot of valuable lessons about life. He taught me the five P's of life; Proper Preparation Prevents Poor Performances so prepare properly. I was in prison when I realized I lacked serious vision for my life. *"Where there is no vision, the people perish; but he that keepeth the law happy is he."* **Proverbs 29:18** The same verse in the NIV reads, *"Where there is no revelation, people cast off restraint; but blessed is the one who heeds wisdom's instruction."*

I used the time I spent in prison to become more educated. I enrolled in the GED program and aced the practice test on the first try. I told the instructor I didn't need the practice test anymore. I was ready for the real thing.

The instructor asked, "Are you sure? It usually takes a few tries for a person to be ready for the real test."

I said, "Bring it on." So the next day, he obliged me and gave me the real GED test. I made high passing scores on each part.

All the instructor could do was to look at me in awe. He shook his head in disbelief. He said, "I have never seen anything like this. Out of all the years I have been doing this course, inside of this jail, you are the first inmate I have ever seen pass the GED on the first try. Many can barely read or write when they get to me. Most of the inmates that come to me can barely spell their name. I have had a few who could not tell time. Son, you are blessed. You are gifted and very intelligent. You do not belong in here. You need to get out of here and do something with your life." I commonly hear and see the negativity around me, so it took someone speaking positivity into me to help me realize I could do better.

After that point, I was very encouraged. My creativity seriously flowed. Imagine being locked up for two years and the main thing you did was write gospel music? That is what I did. The Holy Spirit grabbed me and convicted me. God caused a shift in my spirit and I started to change. I felt bad about all the people I'd hurt. I started to read and meditate on God's word, day and night. God freed me from so much.

Once, I went to jail for four years. One of my sisters introduced me to this girl named Sheila. I didn't know her but she knew my mother and was a friend of the family. She was very kind to me, at first. She visited me and put money on my books. She brought me clothes. When I got out, we were involved for a time. I came out of work release with $16,000. I bought a car and put it in her name. She thought it was a good idea to wait until my license was clear, then the title could be transferred to my name. The set up was short lived. Six months later, I was back out on the streets again. I went on a two-day binge smoking crack. I came back home to get the car I bought. She snitched on me (*I don't like snitches*). She called the police but I got away. I assured her if I see her, I would slap her, and I did. I also told her if I see the car, I would slash the tires and break the windows. Fearing for her safety, she put a restraining order on me but I was not moved by that. I tried to smash her but too many people were around. She took all of my clothes and I tried to beat her down like a man for stealing from me. She ended up letting the car get impounded, which was cool with me. She finally moved far away. My anger used to get the best of me but I thank God for deliverance.

I FOUND MY BLOOD BROTHERS
Chapter Ten

Momma's death took a lot out of me. It weakened me but at the same time, it strengthened me. Through her death, The Lord showed me I had to start doing better in my life in order to receive the blessings He had for me. Momma's death left me broken. *"The Lord is close to the brokenhearted."* **Psalms 34:18 (NIV)** When you are broken, Jesus is right there waiting to comfort you. I know Momma wanted me to live better and thrive.

After I came out of prison, uniquely, I had opportunities to work at a car dealership with two of my childhood friends. I loved playing with them. They were brothers and they lived across the street from us. Although my family moved from the house, I managed to keep in touch with them.

One of the brothers, Pete, Jr., and I, looked so much alike, people called us twins. Pete Jr. told me the stories of his father, Pete Sr., being a real pimp back in the day.

Pete told his father about me, so one day, Pete, Sr., came to the dealership to meet me. Pete said, "Dad, this is Thomas Morrison, Jr. A lot of people say we look alike. Thomas, this is Pete, Sr., my father."

As he walked up to me, he looked closely at me. He said, "Is your mother's name Karen?"

I said, "Yes, you knew my mom?"

His eyes got really big. He said, "Oh man, her husband at the time was my best friend. Man, I seriously need to talk to you, young man."

I said, "About what?"

Pete Sr. said, "It is seriously deep. Can I take you to lunch?"

Pete, J., said, "This better not be what I think this is."

I just had the strangest feeling my life was about to change. I went to speak with the dealership manager and said, "Pete's dad is here. He wants to take me to lunch. I have a weird and awkward feeling he is about to tell me something which would blow my mind away."

The manager said, "That's cool. Are you alright?" I told him I was going to be ok.

We went to a barbeque joint up the street. He said, "This should have come out a long time ago but we vowed not to say anything about it. We didn't want to start no mess between two families, being that we lived right across the street from each other (The Morrison's and the Joneses). I was with your momma the night that Thomas took my car to go to the store to go get more liquor. It was snowing outside. Thomas ended up totaling my car and went to jail for 6 days. Over those 6 days, your mom and I had sex multiple times. When she got pregnant, we swore to tell no one. So all this time, Thomas thought you were his son, but in actuality, you are really my son."

I was totally shocked but not completely surprised. I didn't have a relationship with Thomas Morrison. Somehow, he knew I wasn't his son.

Pete Sr. also said, "No matter what you do in your life, the truth will systematically come out."

That's why I was pretty bold back in the day. If I was going to have another girl on the side, sell drugs or whatever, I told them. I didn't hide. I said, "You mean to tell me *YOU* are my real dad?"

He said, "Yes son, I am."

I said, "What are the odds of me going to work at a dealership with a dude who looks just like me just to find out we are brothers?"

Pete, Sr. just starts crying and apologizing.

A month went by. Pete Sr. and I got tested and it was a positive match. Pete, Sr. was my father. All this time, Pete, Jr. and Chuck were my brothers. My mind was totally blown. I now have five brothers. We all have the same father but different moms. My sisters and I have the same mother but different fathers.

Honestly, at times I wonder why I didn't find out about my father until I was a grown man. One of the crucial aspects of believing in God is He has His timing for everything. His thoughts are above ours. I couldn't understand it then but I am glad it happened. My father accepted me as his son. It was part of my redemption. It was Thomas Morrison's loss for his rejection towards me. I was not the one at fault, he was.

Another part of believing in God is forgiveness. You have to be able to forgive. I had to do this so I could start the healing process and move forward. When you are meant to be a minister in Christ, He takes you through some hard but valuable lessons.

THE RELATIONSHIP FROM HELL
Chapter Eleven

While I was in those streets, I was moved by my fleshly desires and cravings. I craved drugs, alcohol and fast money and I chased women. I got what I wanted, when I wanted it, and that was all that mattered. That behavior affected my relationships greatly with my ex-wives, ex-girls and babies' mommas. All of these women took me through some type of problem. I freely admit that a lot of what happened in my marriages happened because of my drug habits and unfaithfulness.

After Momma passed away, and the Lord came into my life, I wanted to make new and positive changes in my life, but there were some old habits I had let go. One of those bad habits was choosing women. When I was outside prison walls, I couldn't go without a woman for long. As soon as I got rid of one, I was ready to get another. It became an endless cycle. I kept doing that for years, until I broke the cycle with the love of my life. It took a process to get to her. The reason why I didn't find her sooner is because she was hidden in Jesus. A lot of times, when you profess Jesus, and still live like you never knew him, you will learn some hard lessons. My hard lessons came in the shape of a few women. Some of them caused me to have some serious trust issues when I stopped dealing with them because of the lies and deceit.

I thought dealing with the women I was not married to was lesson enough but I was wrong. I had been involved with many women but I didn't get married until much later. I thought when I got married, things would be ok. Man, was I ever wrong. My first wife, Terri, was just one example of my poor judgment. That marriage was one of the worst I had ever experienced in my life. Against my better judgement, I let my guard down, though there were small signs warning me not to get involved with her.

I remember the day I met her. Everything was going great at work. I was making a lot of sales and I was banking a lot of cash. She was a car saleswoman at the dealership I worked at and she was eye candy. She wasn't like the other women I dealt with. There was just something different about her. I loved her confidence. She had an alluring smile and I had to make her mine. I tried to do things right in the sight of the Lord. *"Marriage is honorable in all and the bed undefiled, but whoremongers and adulterers, God will judge."* **Hebrews 13:4**

She became my wife. Every day with her was like the Fourth of July because she knew what to do to stroke my flames. She made me weak in the knees. We were so in love and she was such a sweet woman, at first. She could sweet talk me into anything; after all, she was a saleswoman. I could unwind with her and I could drink and smoke weed with her too. She was incredible, or so I thought. I could not wait to get home to be with her.

The first couple of years were incredible, but then things started to fall apart. No marriage is perfect and sometimes when you meet someone, they are not there to be with you forever. They are there to teach you valuable lessons. All that glitters is *not* gold.

Everything seemed to go wrong in our lives after she went through a brief illness. I went with her on doctor's appointments. She made it through the illness physically, but she seemed to take a different turn mentally after the sickness. It seemed as though she went from being very sweet to being very bitter. She started drinking and smoking weed more heavily. When she got drunk, she become very belligerent and irritable. This girl throw blows like a man. I literally had to bob and weave to defend myself from her powerful punches. She had become a different person from the woman I married.

Then she started instigating fights. We truly had some knock- down, drag out fights. We got to the level of the "break-up to make-up" phase. That was great for a while but our problems started to spill over into the workplace. She threw caution to the wind by picking fights with me on the job; and not all were discreet quarrels. Some were in front of co-workers and customers. I received plenty of warnings from management. I made them a lot of money as a salesman, but they had an image to uphold and our bickering was bad for business and bad for us.

The stress Terri caused me was overwhelming and I began using drugs heavily. I started binging again. I disappeared for two to three days at a time. In exchange for drugs, I let drug dealers use cars for a few hours. I was known to drive a car off the lot, disappearing from the jobsite for two or more hours. I got a hotel room and used the time the dealer was gone, to get a hooker and use drugs, and no one was the wiser. However, I knew and more importantly, God knew. My relationship with Terri became very difficult, both personally and professionally.

After the three-year mark, everything seemed to go from bad to worse in our relationship. When we fought, she'd call the cops on me; though she started the fight in the first place. The cops told me to leave. When that blew over, the fights got even more violent. One day she picked a fight with me and drew a rifle on me.

I yelled, "Put the rifle down." Minutes later, an entire police tactic team came to the house.

She put on quite a performance that night. When the authorities arrived, she told the police it was I who held the rifle on her. She continued with she was scared and feared for her life. Her daughters, who heard the entire thing, tried to convince the police it was their mom who had the gun but they didn't listen. This time, I was led away from the house in handcuffs, and because I was an ex-felon who was not supposed to have a gun, I went to jail and had to serve time for felony possession of a firearm.

I was sentenced to one year in jail. I lost my job at the dealership…and if that wasn't enough, she put a restraining order on me. I served my time in a camp setting. I worked in the kitchen so I ate very well.

When I was released, I was homeless and staying in a shelter. It was a terrible time for me because Terri's lies and schemes set me back greatly. The restraining order wasn't a problem because I didn't want to be in the same room with her or breathe the same air she was breathing and I had no problem staying away from her.

We were equally at fault for our marriage crumbling. Her children were traumatized because of the fighting that went on between us. I regret putting them through the drama.

We were both doing wrong. I was doing a lot of cocaine and alcohol and she was drinking and smoking large amounts of weed. Terri had it out for me. She still wanted revenge even after

I served a year in jail because of her lies. Well she got her revenge when my biological father passed away.

When dad passed away, I was all set to attend the funeral and mourn my father. Little did I know Terri used her powers of manipulation on my brother. She made herself the helpless victim in his eyes. On the day of the funeral, my little brother called me and said Terri was coming to the funeral so I could not come since the restraining order was still active. I missed my dad's funeral because of her. Fury is a gentle word to describe my emotions that day. I was literally thrown aback that she had the nerve to attend my father's funeral. However my mindset changed. Instead of pouting at home, I decided to go to work in North Carolina.

Terri took her revenge to a more sinister level. She lied to my younger brother about everything that happened between us. Although we were both to blame for all of our marital problems, she made it seem as if it were all my fault. My brother ate a plate full of gullible and fell for her lies.

On the day I was paying my respects to my deceased father. I found out that Terri was sleeping with my brother. I was completely devastated and beyond angry with both of them.

The day after the funeral, I violated the restraining order. I went right to our house and I took my frustrations and anger out on her. I beat her up because she slept with my brother. I could not bring myself to forgive her for a very long time. When God doesn't want you to be with a certain person, things will happen to let you know the two of you were not meant to be together. I gladly went to jail when the cops were called. Being married to her was one of the biggest mistakes of my life.

MY OTHER MISTAKES
Chapter Twelve

My second biggest mistake soon followed. Back in the day, I had countless one-night stands. That lifestyle was another kind of crazy. After I won the rap battles in the clubs, women were ready to go home with me. I can't remember all of their names. Many of them were just like me, constantly searching for a piece of kindness and for a good feeling, at least for a few moments. I was desperate most of the time.

The shortest marriage I had was to a woman named May. The marriage lasted one week. I should have known something was wrong because it all just happening too fast.

When I met her, sparks flew, but something seemed to be off. It was as if she was rushing much too fast to get really serious. She honestly pushed the idea of getting married too fast. Our courtship was just a blur.

We quickly got married. The ceremony seemed to be a blur. The reception was a blur. We took our honeymoon on a cruise ship. I was excited to go away with my new bride. I was excited about a new start in my life, but she acted funny the entire time. She acted sick during most of the cruise. She said she thought she was pregnant. I was happy, but thought it was too fast for her to be pregnant. She stayed in the room while I was enjoying myself. I was meeting new people, swimming and eating good food. I did a lot of stuff. I wasn't about to waste money and not enjoy the cruise. I went back and forth to the room checking on her. A couple of times when I returned to the room, she wasn't there. Of course she often had an excuse. She said she was going back and forth trying to get some club soda or something from the bar to settle and relieve her stomach. I told her I could have gotten that for her but she said she needed to get out and get some air.

When we got off the boat things seemed a little more normal, but she was still a bit distracted.

A few days after we got home, everything seemed to be fine and she was feeling much better. Days later May's mom popped up unexpectedly for visit. My mother-in-law was a devout Christian, and the language she used to describe her daughter had me blown away. She came right and said, "My daughter's a whore, my daughter is a whore." She continued to repeat herself quite a few times. She continued the conversation with, "I don't lie. I tried to be honest and you have to know the truth."

What was she trying to tell me about her daughter, my new bride? When May's mother gave me the skinny about the honeymoon cruise, it became apparently clear about May's behavior during our honeymoon. May's mother told me her daughter bought a ticket for a former boyfriend to be (with her) on the cruise ship. She packed more than lingerie and a toothbrush for the honeymoon; she packed a man; her ex! …and had a rendezvous with him on the ship! Who would be that low to do a devilish thing of marrying up and reach back to an ex-lover? That truthfully blew me away. I was beyond shocked and devastated! I was rocked to the very core. If her mother hadn't told me, I would've never known, and May would've gotten away with it.

My anger seriously got the best of me. I punched her as if she was a man. She broke my heart. I was so disappointed in her. What she did was beyond what I could comprehend.

I was trying to do right. I had been faithful to her. After the unexpected leash of emotion resulting in a lashing on May, I thought I might feel better; when in actuality I was numb to near death. She was crying from embarrassment and saying how she was sorry over and over again. Her "*sneak a playah*" onboard completely outweighed and overrode any form of apology she could have for me. It was wasted time and wasted tears. I had NO forgiveness. I was so mad I called the cops on myself. When the cops arrived, I told them exactly what happened. I told them we just got married and I found out that she had snuck another man on to the cruise ship that we were honeymooning on. She made me feel like such a fool.

I told the cops, "We were on our honeymoon on the cruise ship but she acted funny the entire time; acted like she was sick. She said she might be pregnant. Then when we got back home and I found out my wife's ex-boyfriend was on the cruise ship too and she was sleeping with him on the ship. In fact, she bought him the ticket! All of this happened right under my nose! I would never have known this if her mother hadn't told me."

The cops look at each other and said, "She deserved it." They told me to pack my stuff and leave immediately. I happily obliged and drove all that night to get to the next city. Needless to say, the marriage was annulled. Again, I was homeless with nowhere to go. The stress and betrayal led to me to relapse once again. I was tormented and heart broken.

Amy, a new fling, was a devil in disguise. I wasn't actually married to her but the involvement with her was significant, to say the least. I thought she had my best interest at heart because she offered me an opportunity to further myself as a car salesman. She later betrayed me.

It turns out this woman was very messed up. She was seriously hooked on methamphetamines. That was why her teeth looked so bad. She was a good-looking woman but over time, her appearance slowly deteriorated. To top it all off, I found out she was sleeping around on me with her own brother. When I found out she was sleeping with her own brother, I was disgusted with her. She tried to seduce me but I wouldn't hear it. She got very angry at me and wanted to fight me. Then she got revenge on me. She called the cops crying and carrying on, saying I was trying to kill her. She accused me of sticking a pistol in her mouth. She told those lies because I refused to sleep with her.

They arrested me. I prayed when I got to my cell because if they found me guilty of attempted murder, I'd be back in jail for a very, very long time. After I prayed about the matter, and the Lord gave me a strategy. He gave me the wisdom to outsmart her. I thought about DNA that had come a very long way. I never put the gun in her mouth. The gun wasn't even mine. After all the mess she had put me through, I still cared about her. She was one of the few people to give me a second chance. I wouldn't have done that to her.

At my hearing, the judge was telling me how he felt about the matter. I swore again to the judge that I hadn't put the gun in her mouth. I asked the judge to do a DNA test on the pistol to see if I was lying. Low and behold, the test did not show any of my DNA on the pistol and I became a free man.

Lilly was another mistake. She was just as guilty as I was for our failed relationship. She and I slept around on each other. We truly weren't committed together. When she became pregnant, of course I doubted paternity, but as fate would have it, the child was mine. We took the DNA test and as a result, I looked like the one to blame, when both of us were at fault. My child and I have a strained relationship but I pray that changes.

ADDICTIONS
Chapter Thirteen

I had to dedicate an entire chapter to discuss my addictions, especially after talking about the birth of my baby girl. *"Can two walk together unless they agree?"* **Amos 3:3** The failure that happened in this next relationship was completely my fault. After I left jail for fighting Terri, I found myself on the road working again. Instead of going after Christ, I kept bingeing on drugs to soothe the pain. In this next relationship, I was my own worst enemy.

We started off in a homeless shelter. I had just gotten there. When I got to this new town, I tried getting on my feet by finding a place stay. Rebecca was a beautiful girl and I was attracted to her immediately. There was something about her that made me want to be with her and take care of her. In a short time, we became extremely close. We fell in love, and within a few months, Rebecca became pregnant with our baby girl. I worked seriously hard at the dealership and bought us a house in a very nice town.

Everything seemed to be right, but as time went on, I relapsed again. There was a constant strain on our relationship by being consistently inconsistent. I went on binges for several days. There was no communication; Rebecca didn't know if I were dead or alive. When I decided to come home, I drove right into a roadblock. The police was on my trail. It was not a good day because I had all the things one is NOT supposed to have in a moving vehicle. I had crack. I was also rolling a joint and had an open container. I tried to get away by turning down a side street but when I tried to avoid the block, the cops quickly followed me. As they closed in on me, I ran right into a dead-end road. It was a done deal. I was arrested on the spot. In my possession, I had $2200, a crack pipe, and a wine bottle. When I got out of jail, my belongings, my girl, and our baby were all gone. My initial reaction was to blame her for leaving and taking my child. I felt so betrayed. How could she take my daughter and leave me? I felt she left me for dead. She did not stand by me. But the truth of the matter was she left because she did not want to be with a drug addict.

The multiple and overpowering addictions to drugs, sex, money and anger was the culprit to many failed relationships. I had three failed marriages because I allowed the demonizing habits of drugs and domestic violence take over. I was married to the addiction more than to the women. I was unreasonably angry with my wives, but never unfaithful to the appetites of my flesh. I stayed in the clubs doing rap contests. I was savage when it came to competition. I thrived on competing against rappers whom I considered phony.

Women love a winner. As soon as I won a rap contest, they were ready to line up to take "the prize" home. Back in the mid 80's and 90's, I had innumerable one-night stands from the clubs that I couldn't keep track of them all. The many soul ties were made with women, but all out of insatiable hunger in the spirit of drug use which led me to arrest and nearly losing my life many times. I didn't consider the consequence; I was only interested in the score. So I lied, stole, and cheated to get anything I needed.

Once when I was homeless, I was desperate for money. I

ripped some yellow pages out of a phone book and rubbed them on the on the pavement; the dirty pavement where people had been walking and spiting on all day. I cut up the dirty pages and stood on the corner, waiting on a mark. I lucked up. Oftentimes, desperation on the streets can pay off for the street hustler.

Some desperate college students were looking for some weed and stopped. I was able to sell them yellow pages I had made dirty by dragging them on the pavement. It was a quick $50 and I left that corner as soon as I made the sale. That's the kind of stuff I did in desperation.

When I was on a binge, I slept on benches or under the interstate overpass. I was following in my mom's footsteps. She went on binges for days and slept anywhere she could. I slept in cardboard boxes in alleys. I stood on the corner panhandling and begging for money, only to take that money to go buy crack. I was angry. I stayed to myself. I was so broken, especially when I went to jail. A lot of regret set in.

To those whom I hurt, I apologize. I wasn't the person then that God has called me to be now, and I am thankful to God because He didn't hold my sins against me but forgave me.

Sexual addictions come from the lust of the eyes, lust of the flesh and the pride of life; these three things will cause you to miss God. Who will you serve? *We cannot serve two masters; we cannot serve God and mammon.* **(Matthew 6:24)** Life is a choice, please choose wisely. Eternity is a very long time to pay for something we did in our lives while on earth.

I know from experience lust and pride will get you into so much trouble. These things make you go after things which are not good for you. No one could tell me anything. If I wanted something, I didn't stop until I got it in my hand. The love of money will make you walk the streets at night and risk your life.

God can blow your mind with a complete turnaround. The pimp is not your friend. It is best to run from him and never look back. It is never too late for you to make your life right. It won't be easy at first. When you are making money legally, it can often come much slower. *"Dishonest money dwindles away, but whoever gathers money little by little makes it grow."* **Proverbs 13:11 (NLT)** The money you make through legal means is a lot more rewarding. Many times David gave in to his fleshly desires. David was anointed to be king of Israel while he was just a little boy. David loved God. Even while David was a little boy, he played instruments to God. He sang and wrote music for the Lord (sounds like someone I know). David praised the Lord God so much one day, he danced right out of his clothes. That was some heavy praising.

David knew when he had done wrong. When he sinned, he was on his face praying and asking God for forgiveness. To me, the story of David is one of the most significant stories in the Bible. David was a mighty fighting man. He fought valiantly in war.

David consulted God on many things, but he had an insatiable lust for many women. One woman was just not enough. One of the biggest mistakes he ever made was while he just happened to be on his roof, taking an evening stroll (this is how most men get in trouble; they luck up on something during a midnight stroll). While he was taking his stroll, he just happened to glance over the rooftops, only to see a woman, by herself, taking an evening bath. He saw her and he had to have her, so he sent one of his servants to get the woman. Her name was Bathsheba and she was the wife of Uriah, one of his most loyal soldiers.

However, David didn't care about Uriah's loyalty. All David was focused on was his wife's beauty and how she should be David's; regardless of the circumstance or consequence. She was brought to David and he slept with her. You can only imagine things just snowballed from there.

In order to cover up the pregnancy, David tried to send her husband Uriah back home to her so he could lay down with his wife. It was said that it was his baby. Uriah was loyal to the army so he did not lay with his wife as he was ordered. David put him on the front line and Uriah was killed.

David and Bathsheba were married. When the baby boy was born, he was very sick. David fasted and prayed before God for the baby to be healed, but the baby died. Even after the baby died, David accepted God's judgment, but God forgave David. He allowed David and Bathsheba to have another son named Solomon, who became was the wisest king to ever walk the earth.

My point of discussing David is this, even though David was wrong in every regard, he made sure to have a relationship with God. David wasn't by any means a perfect man. David acknowledged, over and over, in the book of Psalm how much he needed God. He made it a point to pray, worship, and repent when he was wrong. In return, God promised him an heir to the throne of glory (*see 2 Samuel 7:12-17 and Isaiah 11:10*).

RELAPSE
Chapter Fourteen

As I mentioned earlier, there were often many pitfalls in my journey to get sober and clean. Staying clean and sober were constant struggles for me. A lot of times I took two steps forward just to take eight steps back. As I got my life together, lots of people believed in me. Doors I could not imagine began opening up for me. However, it was like a stronghold was over me because I felt I could never get it right for anything in the world. Temptation was around every corner, waiting to trip me up and make me fall on my face, but I thank God for forgiving me. He is the God of many chances. He knows us because He created us in His image. Invariably, we let him down with our behavior and lifestyle.

Sins are bad and causes us to want what we want without regard to the consequences that follow. When the Israelites were freed from Egypt, they had to struggle to get free of the old behaviors. When you study **Exodus, Leviticus** and much of the **New Testament**, it was a constant struggle for them to get through things. There were times when they said it was better for them to be back in Egypt.

At times we allow ourselves to be pulled back into bondage. When the devil wants you, he will send temptation in nice packages. It could be the woman, in my case, who gave me a second chance at getting it right. I thought she was helping me, but later found out she was in bondage herself. I thought this woman was clean. I thought this woman was pure in her intentions, but little did I know she was the devil in disguise; she was a temptress. She was beautiful. Don't you know a lot of times your greatest enemy will come neatly packaged as someone who seems to have your best interest at heart? She lured me with her beauty; the beauty of her kindness just swept me in. I didn't see her coming. She seduced me so incredibly. I was supposed to have my defenses up. I was supposed to be on my guard. She played her role very well. Her mask came off at the last moment. In the meantime, my flesh got the best of me. My guard was down.

I found myself alone in a hotel suite with her. When the time came, she paid for the suite. The suite had a kitchen, living room and bedroom with a king size bed. I met her there at the hotel. Although she was helping me, I often fantasized about being with her. When we were behind closed doors, we wasted no time. We got undressed. Everything quickly got hot and heavy. She pulled away from me. She got up and went to her purse. She pulled out something familiar. It was a bag filled with crack rocks. She poured the crack rocks onto the table. She pulled out a pipe and lighter. We looked at each other. She pulled me back into relapse, but I was at fault. I was not innocent in the matter.

Although I called myself a child of the Most High God, I did not live like one. I hungered and thirsted for the things of the world. I was still looking for those temporary highs through sex, drugs, and even flattery. This encounter had all of the things the old me desired and craved. There we were, in the hotel suite. We had sex and smoked crack. Two days went by and depression had set in. My heart and my body were hurting. It was part of an ongoing cycle. I still do not understand to this day how a chemical could completely deplete my finances. I had the power to stop it but I didn't.

Overtime, we kept up the rendezvous. We met at our spot, had sex and smoked crack every time we got paid, until there was nothing left. It all became routine. I finally got tired of it. I realized the temptress had led me back down a dark road. I was on this dark road before. It wasn't completely her fault; I was a willing participant. I allowed myself to go down that dark road to be deceived by Satan. *"Lest Satan should get an advantage of us, for we are not ignorant of his schemes." 2nd* **Corinthians 2:11** *When you call yourself a child of God, beware. You have to stay on your guard at all times. "Now those who belong to Christ Jesus have crucified the flesh with its passions and desires."* **Galatians 5:24**

I had money, prestige, material wealth, I had it all. I realized it doesn't matter about your social status, drugs will keep the elite such as doctors, lawyers, basketball stars, musicians, politicians, and men of God in such deep bondage to sin. I, like they were powerless in attempts to break free. There had to be more to life than checking into a hotel and smoking crack, and I wanted it. I wanted a new life without fleeting moments or downward roads.

I'd come to my wits end. Enough was enough. I was tired of being sick and tired. I chose to resist the devil and flee. I quit my job, sold a lot of things I had, packed up the rest of my belongings, and left. I didn't utter a word to her of my plans to leave. I drove as far away as I could get. I left behind the pain, the misery, the shame, and I asked God to forgive me for falling prey again.

I found myself in some rural area. For a while, I didn't tell anyone where I was from. I stayed pure in my body, mind, and spirit. I worked hard. My new lifestyle was a total shock to some who knew me. I sought the face of the Lord. He was the first person I talked to in the morning and the last person I talked to at night. I prayed and read the Word. I took long walks with Him. I wanted to please God and live a life upright before Him. I found myself, in this new place selling cars. All of a sudden, I met the most beautiful woman I'd ever seen in my life. When I met her, I just knew she was going to be my wife. As I got to know her, I found she was just as beautiful on the inside as she was on the outside.

Faith was the vehicle to allow God to send me the mate He designed just for me. Up until this point, all the other women I'd ever been involved with, I depended solely on my flesh to choose. The difference between every other woman and her is God chose her for me. Allowing God to bless me in such a profound way was a sign I was finally becoming free to trust His way. The Lord confirmed my feelings as I prayed specifically about the matter. However, a spirit of self-sabotaging came over me. It was a familiar spirit I was used to. I succumbed to its vices and it caused me to relapse again.

Like a fish on a rod with the hook in mouth, I was quickly pulled in. I should have used wisdom to pull back and say no to its influences.

Tonya is a real God-fearing woman. I had to make a conscience choice. While disclosing my feelings about all the things I had done, she let me know, without inhibitions, she was NOT going to compete with alcohol and drugs.

> *"No servant can serve two masters for he will hate one and love the other or else he will hold the one and despise the other you cannot serve God and Mammon."* **Luke 16:13**

This woman has great faith. She feared and loved Christ. She ministered to me with her whole heart through her faith, love and reverence. Her relationship with the Lord was so deep, I knew I had to get to know God stronger through her lifestyle. This was definitely a game changer! She had a big heart, but she refused to compromise. She was not about to put up with that old man and his old ways. She demanded I stop doing the drugs, stop drinking alcohol and become serious about my life, if I wanted to be with her. She saw so much more in me than I ever saw in myself. She wanted so much more from me than all of the other women I'd been with. Former relationships kept me in enslaved to dysfunction.

Tonya was unmoved by my honesty about my criminal record, history of domestic violence, or drug use; she loved me through it and stood by me. It blest me that she accepted me as I was. The relapse was a familiar thing. I was afraid of messing up yet again. *"Without faith, it is impossible to please God." – **Hebrews 11: 6*** It took faith for me to move forward into the unknown. Now I have Heaven on Earth. She is flesh of my flesh and bone of my bone. She supports me in every endeavor. Mrs. Tonya Morrison I will surely love you forever and ever.

Walking with God is often uncomfortable and uncertain, but I promise you, it is so worth it. No matter what you have done, you do have time to get it right. God is a forgiving God. You can start over with a clean slate. The first key to change is you must confess your sins to Him and submit to Him. *"If we say we have no sins, we deceive ourselves and the truth is not in us. If we confess our sins, God is faithful to forgive our sins and cleanse us from all unrighteousness." – **1 John 1:9***

I was a pimp, a drug-head, an adulterer, a thief, and I was almost a murderer. I was also double-minded. Growing in God, I've discovered confession is good food for the soul. Confession leads to honesty and honesty leads to change. This time, because I TRULY let the Lord into my life, I changed. Those former things that used to entice me no longer fulfill me.

EPILOGUE
My Final Thoughts

Darkness and light does not mix. When they do, the light overcomes the darkness. I read the Word, and I have been praying and pursuing a relationship with God. I am not that same man who was fulfilled by drug infused flings. My spirit has changed. When you start chasing God, be prepared. A lot of those old ways will no longer fulfill you. I wanted so much more. I got tired of empty sexual encounters. I got tired of how drugs tore my personal and professional relationships apart.

It is now time for you, the person reading this book, to make some decisions. The old way is no longer sufficient. It is time for you to make a new start. In order to experience those new things, I had to die to my old self, and that was one of the hardest things I've ever had to do. I had to die to the way I did things of the world. It was a tough thing to do but I did it.

I also had to change that poverty mindset. The poverty mindset wants to hold on to everything that is tangible. That mindset will have you holding on to things that do not last. Millions upon millions lose out every day because they have that poverty mindset.

Like many of you, at my core, I was a businessman. I just had to shift my focus and become a legitimate businessman so I could make it on the outside of the prison system. I made the decision that I'd had enough of the prison life and I was never going back or looking back. I also used my prison time much more productively. Most of the time, I sat in my cell and wrote more rap music. When I died to my old self, my rap lyrics started to change. I went from rapping about selling drugs to rapping about salvation and how to find God. I became very committed to Christian living. I started studying the Word of God for myself to truly understand the meaning of salvation and redemption.

It took years of circumstances, trials, tests, and tribulations to get to where I am now. When you are working towards your dreams, you may fail. People will let you down. You may let yourself down, like I did. If I had let go of the kilo situation, I would have been very successful in the secular rap world right now, but God has a reason for everything. People will tell you no when you need them the most, but don't let that deter you. There are some positive people in this world who will support and encourage you to your next level up.

You will fall down but the goal is to pick yourself up and keep going. Whether you are trying to succeed in the rap game, succeed in school, succeed in marriage, parenthood, or succeed in life, you must keep striving; even when the odds are stacked against you. After three failed marriages, I could have given up on marriage and missed out on meeting the love of my life. God strengthened me and guided me and He can do the same for you.

You can read a book all day, but the main person who has to want to change is you. You have to take action and move forward. I pray you will move forward and fulfill your destiny.

FOCUS SCRIPTURE

1 Corinthians 13: 4-5 Love is patient, love is kind, it does not envy, it does not boast, it is not proud, it does not dishonor others, it is not self-seeking, it is not easily angered, it keeps no record of wrong doing.

MORE ABOUT THE AUTHOR

Thomas L. Morrison, III is a native of Seattle, Washington. He has an eclectic life as entrepreneur, a national recording artist, and minister of the Gospel.

Morrison is a passionate individual who puts his heart and soul on the line for his wife and his children.

He enjoys witnessing, preaching, family time, and music. His stage name is the Sanktified Soulja, and he is known throughout the USA as a recording RAP artist in the Gospel/Christian Rap arena.

www.ingramcontent.com/pod-product-compliance
Lightning Source LLC
Chambersburg PA
CBHW021957290426
44108CB00012B/1103